WITHDRAWN BY THE
UNIVERSITY OF MICHIGAN

The Alien in Their Midst

Manasseh ben Israel, Dutch rabbi who facilitated the Jews' readmission to England in 1656.

The Alien in Their Midst

Images of Jews in English Literature

Esther L. Panitz

SARA F. YOSELOFF MEMORIAL PUBLICATIONS
In Judaism and Jewish Affairs

This volume is one in a series established in memory
of Sara F. Yoseloff,
who devoted her life to the making of books.

Rutherford ● Madison ● Teaneck
Fairleigh Dickinson University

London and Toronto: Associated University Presses

© 1981 by Associated University Presses, Inc.

Associated University Presses, Inc.
4 Cornwall Drive
East Brunswick, New Jersey 08816

Associated University Presses
69 Fleet Street
London EC4Y 1EU, England

Associated University Presses
Toronto M5E, Canada

Library of Congress Cataloging in Publication Data

Panitz, Esther L
   The alien in their midst.

   Bibliography: p.
   Includes index.
   1. English literature--History and criticism.
2. Jews in literature. I. Title
PR151.J5P3   820'.9'35203924   78-75183
ISBN 0-8386-2318-2

Printed in the United States of America

Contents

Acknowledgments
Introduction
1 The Blood Libel   23
2 Venice and Belmont   42
3 Jews and Right Reason   64
4 Jews and Middle-Class Culture   81
5 Fagin and Philistinism   103
6 Alienation and the Cult of the Individual   127
7 Summary   162
    Notes   171
    Bibliography   181
    Index   192

To
Zimra Koko,
Aaron Obadiah,
and Yasmeen Alexis
with love

Acknowledgments

I am indebted to Cecil Roth, Salo W. Baron, and James Parkes for their understanding of the Jewish historical experience. Critical comprehensions of the early, medieval, and renaissance periods of English literature that characterize the work of Hijman Michelson, Jacob Lopes Cardozo, Myer Jack Landa, and Hermann Sinsheimer have served as essential guides in developing the thesis of this book. Harm Reijndert Sientjo Van Der Veen and Edgar Rosenberg have illuminated the roles Jews have played in eighteenth century English literature and have stressed their stereotypical images in both drama and fiction, with Rosenberg's extending the pattern in English fiction until the beginning of the twentieth century. I am grateful to both of these authors for their analyses, as I am to Harold Fisch who in his work emphasized the good Jew and the bad Jew as types in English literature. The benefits to be derived from an overall perspective achieved by David Philipson and Montagu Frank Modder have proved most beneficial. The number of authors cited here is by no means exclusive of the many others whose varied understandings of the Jew in English literature have contributed to the development of *The Alien in Their Midst*. Needless to add, I alone am responsible for any errors in fact or judgment.

I should like to thank the following publishers for permission to quote from the sources listed:

The Alien in Their Midst

From *Dover Beach* by Matthew Arnold, *English Poets, Romantic Victorian and Later*, copyright 1933, The American Book Co.

From *Ulysses* by James Joyce published by The Bodley Head: From *Ulysses* by James Joyce. Copyright 1914, 1918, by Margaret Caroline Anderson and renewed 1942, 1946 by Nora Joseph Joyce. Reprinted by permission of Random House, Inc.

From *The Diary of Samuel Pepys*. J.M. Dent & Sons Ltd; E.P. Dutton & Co.

From "The Jews," by Henry Vaughn. *The Oxford Book of Seventeenth-Century Verse*. Edited by Sir Herbert Grierson and Geoffrey Bullough. Copyright 1935. Oxford University Press.

From "The Jews," by George Herbert. *Major Metaphysical Poets*. Edited by Oscar Williams. Simon & Schuster.

From *This Gun for Hire* by Graham Greene. Copyright 1936, (c) 1964 by Graham Greene. Reprinted by permission of The Viking Press.

From *This Gun for Hire* by Graham Greene. Published in Britain under the title of *A Gun for Sale* by William Heineman Ltd. and The Bodley Head.

In particular, I am thankful to members of my family, Raphael, Jonathan and Jane, and Michael and Sheila, whose constant encouragement sustained me in my work. Words

Acknowledgments

cannot express the unfailing interest and unflagging devotion extended to me by my husband, David. His constructive ideas helped mold this book and turn it into a reality.

Introduction

The Alien in Their Midst: Images of Jews in English Literature deals with Christian conceptions about Jews. From the fourteenth century to the present, fact and fancy, truth and imagination have all combined to shape a unique image of the Jew in Christian eyes. Variations in thought, wrought by man's changing perceptions, have added to the complexity of the portrait. Yet its basic outlines have not been altered; they proclaimed the alien quality, the strangeness of the Jew. His distinctiveness was allegedly bound to a peculiar emphasis upon the uses of wealth and power.

This essential pattern for fashioning a composite Christian portrait of the Jew as he appears in literature was drawn as early as New Testament times. But this book spans only seven centuries of the nineteen that have elapsed since the beginning of Christianity, and its locale is confined to England. There is no intention here of producing an encyclopedic work dealing with the changing Christian views of Jews in Western literature. During the Anglo-Saxon period the relatively meager references to Jews repeated biases originally expressed in the Gospels. Jews received fuller consideration only after they had settled in Britain at the invitation of William the Conqueror. This work, then, begins with the medieval period and focuses on the story of differing Christian perceptions of Jews to this day.

For the past fifty years the image of the Jew in English

Introduction

literature has been depicted in a variety of ways. Early on, writers were aware that Christians regarded the Jews of the Old Testament in a kindly fashion, but reserved a special animus for their descendants. This is especially true in New Testament references and in later theological commentaries. Other authors have noted the changing fortunes of the Jews at any given time, in their particular relationships to the governing parties in England. Some students in the field have been taken with the inherent paradox in the Christian concept of the Jews. Though they were accused of having betrayed Christ, they had nevertheless to be sustained as living witnesses to the central truth of Christianity. This two-pronged approach led to distinctions between the good and the bad Jew, characterizations that in turn reinforced earlier stereotypical notions of what Jews were supposed to have been. And in the last few decades there has been a considerable amount of research into the nature of just such Jewish archetypes in literature.[1]

The insights gleaned from all these sources have been invaluable in planning this book. Its emphasis, however, derives from another basic theme: as English civilization changed, different economic, social, and political factors altered some of the ideas Christian writers may have held about Jews, but the qualities of distinctiveness and alienation attributed to them have remained constant to this day. From Chaucer's time until the present, various ways of viewing the Jews merely intensified a belief in their racial and religious separateness. It was this quality that enabled the medieval populace to endow them with disgusting physical and spiritual characteristics. As we shall see, the Jews of Chaucer's *Prioresses Tale* were capable of atrocities because they were not like other humans. Even writers of the Renaissance who viewed men as the measure of all things never intended Barabas, the Jew of Malta, or Shylock, the antagonist of *The Merchant of Venice*, to be models for others to follow. Indeed, these two cutthroats were portrayed as bloodthirsty,

THE ALIEN IN THEIR MIDST

demonic userers, fascinated by the uses of power. Only the very peculiarities of their nature could have accounted for their villainy.

During Cromwell's day, when accommodation was made with the Jews for economic reasons, their alienism helped stir age-old movements for their conversion. Still greater emphasis was laid upon the Jews' physical repulsiveness, strange attire, peculiar speech, and general outlandishness in all those witty, and, more frequently, mindless, eighteenth-century plays and novels. Even the later Romantic writers, in dealing with the Jew in literature, based their sentimentalism on the seeming strangeness of his ways.

A refurbished alliance between Jews and wealth in the nineteenth century drew its sustenance from the notion that Jews were still the outcasts of society. During the Renaissance church leaders and lay people had looked on with horror at the presumed affinity of strange Jews with riches and power. But later, in the Victorian era, the Jewish predilection for high finance expanded into dreadful situations in which alien merchant princes and politicians, imitating their forebears' worst behavior, were intent upon controlling the world. Disraelian and Darwinian notions of race fed the imaginations of those writers who saw Jews lurking behind every international conspiracy. Despite her Zionist aspirations, her confirmed belief in the qualitative value of cultural enrichment through different racial and ethnic traits colored George Eliot's writing. Earlier in the century Dickens had set the pace by seeking the paradigm for all his villains in Fagin, the Jew thief of *Oliver Twist*. With Dickens in the lead, William Makepeace Thackeray and Anthony Trollope then rang all the changes upon financial maneuvers, malpractices that were tied, directly or indirectly, to Jews, who were still the mysterious aliens. Sometimes these storied variations upon Jews and wealth were in deadly earnest; on other occasions they were caricatures, intended for comic purposes.

In characteristic fashion, George Bernard Shaw turned this

Introduction

theme on its head when he lauded the benefits millionaire bankers brought to the world. But the association of Jews with heaps of gold survived even Shaw's acerbic pen, to intrigue twentieth-century writers. Despite differences in their personal estimates of Jews, John Galsworthy, Graham Greene, Evelyn Waugh, W. Somerset Maugham, C. P. Snow, and George Orwell were unable to separate the idea of the Jew from the "cash-nexus." Of these, only Galsworthy, Orwell, and Snow hesitated about ascribing human failings to their Jewish protagonists on the basis of wealth and race. Yet even with these writers the suspicion that Jews "got on so" because of their intellectual prowess, or money schemes, or different origins, remained. It was left for James Joyce, the only one of the moderns to do so, to see the Jews merely as human beings. In *Ulysses* he recorded all of Leopold Bloom's personal insufficiencies and ethnic longings without judging him in any way.

Within so overwhelming a context of alienation, it then becomes irrelevant to ask whether anti-Semitism prompted *The Prioresses Tale*, *The Merchant of Venice*, *Oliver Twist*, *The Way We Live Now*, *Brighton Rock*, and all those other selections where the image of the Jew has been darkened beyond recognition. It would seem, however, that in each instance the quality of his difference from the norm that was attributed to the Jew formed the basis for the creation of these literary works.

In selected certain examples to illustrate these developments, I have been guided by several principles. The works referred to in this book are representative pieces whose popular appeal has stood the test of time. Minor authors and their contributions have been resorted to where such examples set the pattern for new literary trends, or best embody a specific outlook in time. To avoid undue repetition, I have on occasion deliberately omitted some of the more hackneyed statements about Jews expressed by well-known authors. Because this study combines a certain amount of economic and intellectual history, and at times relies upon close textual analyses, my choice of literary examples is a selective one.

Their number varies with the centuries. For the medieval period, only Chaucer's *Prioresses Tale* is included, for it serves as a touchstone by which to evaluate the prevailing attitude of the medieval church to the Jews. One of Chaucer's famous contemporaries, John Gower, in his *Confessio Amantis*, does repeat a tale where a clever Jew tricks a heathen, and another, William Langland, of *Piers the Plowman* fame, urges his readers to practice that type of charity which Jews extend to one another.[2] But Gower's story is just another illustration of the views concerning the Jews that were popular at the time, and Langland's reference has left no enduring influence.

Scholars have estimated that of the fifteen hundred or more plays written during the Elizabethan period, a scant nine bear some reference to Jews.[3] Of these, only *The Jew of Malta* and *The Merchant of Venice* are remembered today. The remainder survive mainly as historical material for scholarly investigation, and are therefore not under consideration here.

With the return of the Jews to England in Cromwell's time, their visible presence brought about an increase in the number of literary works pertinent to Jewish matters. This fact alone made it necessary here to expand the range, both in terms of the number of authors to be considered and in the amount and nature of the material they produced. The later chapters of this book are characterized by a multiple coverage of writers and their offerings.

Choosing sources to illustrate the themes of the chapters has been made on the basis of the same criteria. More space is devoted to better-known authors than to minor ones. What John Donne thought about Jews, or Milton's view on certain theological matters, is considered more important than the opinions of other seventeenth-century authors. Similarly, for the eighteenth century, the thoughts of Dryden, Swift, Pope,

Introduction

and the major novelists concerning the Jews carry greater weight than the innumerable allusions by minor dramatists, who mined the same vein of humor, grounded on buffoonery at the Jews' expense. By way of contrast, a more detailed study of Sir Walter Scott's *Ivanhoe* serves as inclusive reference to the development of sentimentalism, with its lightened image of the Jew. The attitude of other Regency novelists toward the Jews has been so meticulously explored elsewhere as to make its repetition here unnecessary.[4] References to the legend of the Wandering Jew are included when relevant to the work at hand, but the Wandering Jew's transformation to a universal bogeyman in the Gothic novel has not been dealt with here. Detailing and evaluating such a change would not properly fit into the scope of this book.

With the exception of Robert Browning, whose psychological insight into Jews and other characters in his dramatic monologues set him apart from his literary colleagues, most prominent Victorian writers thought of Jews in terms of wealth and race. Their views, along with Browning's, have been considered in this study.

There is no attempt here to discuss the works of other well-known authors whose popularity has diminished in the modern period. Edward Lytton Bulwer, Charles Kingsley, Charles Reade, George Meredith, and Dion Boucicalt, who repeated themes of Jews in the Rothschild mold, of Jews and a reformed Christianity, of Jews and the benefits of Socialism, or of just plain, old, rascally Jews, are not included.

Biblical motifs in this book have been alluded to in terms of its major topic, Christian perceptions of Jews. There is no intent here to deal in any detail with novels or poems based on biblical themes. These are universal in scope. Because this work is concerned with attitudes of Christian writers in their literary characterizations of Jews, it would be inappropriate to consider those selections in English fiction and drama by Jewish writers which deal with subjects of Jewish interest.

The Alien in Their Midst

Most of these were published in the nineteenth and twentieth centuries.

During the modern period, George Bernard Shaw, John Galsworthy, Graham Greene, James Joyce, George Orwell, and C. P. Snow had new and varied points of view to express about the Jews. But such novelists as Evelyn Waugh and W. Somerset Maugham merely repeated the usual anti-Semitic clichés. These have been noted in several passing references to their works. T. S. Eliot and Ezra Pound have not been included in this study, for they are American writers, and *The Alien in Their Midst: Images of Jews in English Literature* is limited to the British Isles.

1
The Blood Libel

"I will love what thou lovest; I will hate what thou hatest." "As long as I shall live, I am bound to serve you and respect you." "Thy friends will be my friends, thy enemies my enemies."[1]

THESE separate oaths of vassals to their lords have echoed through the many centuries spanned by the Middle Ages. The loyalties that these pledges signified were the only redeeming factors in untold lives otherwise marked by a total disregard for the worth of the individual. Human life was indeed cheap in a world where warfare among feudal chieftains was an everyday occurence, and where the economic struggle for survival decreed that men were old at thirty. Behind the glittering façades of isolated castles, where these lofty promises were spoken, the human condition was only slightly less precarious for the noble knight swearing fealty to his lord than it was for the townsfolk and serfs dwelling on the lands of the manor. But for the Jews of the Middle Ages life was always being lived on the edge of a precipice.

They were unacceptable to the society on whose periphery they lived. They were ostracized by the Christian majority; the Catholic Church proscribed any social relationships between Christians and Jews, and the Jewish communal structure helped sustain the separateness of the Jews as a group. Furthermore, the Jews were never part of that closed medieval system which ordained that loyalty should flow from the lowly serf upward to the vassal and on to the secular lord himself. For the code of chivalry found its justification in medieval Christianity, a way of life whose philosophic premises were rooted in the elimination of Jews qua Jews, or in their conversion. Both individually and collectively, the Jews in the Middle Ages constituted a palpable evil, beyond the pale of a normative existence. For they had betrayed the Christian Savior, and accordingly were numbered among those evil spirits who found their "tutelary" inspiration in association with the Devil.

Though the Church proclaimed a unitary view of life, with monotheism as its watchword, it nevertheless was a warring institution, prepared to do battle against all opponents, both corporeal and imaginary. In its obsession with an endless conflict between good and evil, the Church associated most of the pernicious, heretical spirits, who were supposed to have the roots of their existence in the Devil, with the Jews. These, it was presumed, were continually arrayed in battle against God, the King, whose warrior was Christ. For this reason, the mass and the sacraments were there to serve as defensive armor for simple Christians in their battle with the netherworld. The priests were to act as counsel in defending the Christian spirit against Satan, who was also the Devil's advocate and representative of the Jews. In the ongoing conflict, it became the obligation of the Church to insure salvation by defeating the Devil, and forcing men to accept the grace of the Christian Savior.[2] But the Jews, it appeared, were stiffnecked and stubborn. Not only did they refuse conversion, except under duress, but they also, by their very nature, could not be fitted into the divinely ordained sequence of existence that Christianity had created. They did not lock into any proper medieval niche. They were not part of the chain of being that ascended either in God's scheme of creation from the lowliest worm to the angels or, in a secular sense, from the worthless serf and villein to the knight or lord. Theologically, they were part of the netherworld; allegiance to the Lord God and, in the Christian sense, to his Son, required those identical virtues which were necessary to sustain a secular lord. But honor, obedience, love of truth, and the pursuit of battle against an earthly foe did not apply to the Jews. In the Middle Ages they were never a part of the communities in which they dwelled. They were regarded as strangers whose periodic physical persecutions and expulsions from the temporary lands of their dispersions were justified. Popular thought had it that like their fiendish Master, they were intent upon destroying the Christian community by any means at their disposal. Among simple Christian folk it was commonplace to assume that Jews poisoned wells, helped spread the Black Death, desecrated the Host, and slaughtered Christian children for arcane religious purposes.

Economically, the Jews were tolerated only as long as their money lasted. Their sufferance rested on their ability to provide available cash for the petty kings and dukes in whose fiefdoms they would be granted temporary refuge. From 1066 until 1290 the Jews moved across the stage of English history only because they served as sources of financial credit to the kings.

The Jews had come to be moneylenders through a combination of historic factors. Centuries of forced exclusion from trade and manufacture, and clerical proscriptions against owning land had taught them the art of living by their wits—of learning to barter and deal only in movable assets. Years of sophisticated urban existence, characterized by high, and highly literate, levels of knowledge, had enabled Jews to turn to the fields of banking and factoring. In practice, the Church's otherworldly dictum that moneylending was an odious occupation fit only for nonbelievers now assured the Jews of a means of existence formally prohibited to Christians. Officially, the Jews were the usurers of the Middle Ages.

It was in this capacity that William the Conquerer invited the Jews in his territory of Rouen, France, to accompany him upon his invasion of England. There are isolated references before the Norman Conquest to the presence of Jews in Britain, but the Jews as a class acquire some significance in the land only after the Norman Conquest. As the fiscal agents of royalty they were essential to the monarchs in sustaining their business ventures, in maintaining their armies, particularly during the Crusades, and in serving as financial pawns in the kings' endless battles with their barons for the division of sovereignty. As the fortunes of each king waxed or waned, so did the future wellbeing—and frequently, the very lives—of the Jews in his domains depend on whether the royal coffers were empty or full, whether the nobility was peaceful or rebellious, whether the country as a whole had had a successful campaign overseas. Such misadventures as marked the first two crusades often spelled impoverishment and torture for English Jewry.[3]

Prior to the Crusades, individual relationships between Christians and Jews were generally peaceful, but with the onset of those bloodbaths, both religious and economic hatred of the Jews intensified. Those anti-Semitic passions unleashed by the zeal of the Crusader knights on the way to Jerusalem filtered down to the common people, so that during this period all the roads to the Holy Land were soaked with the blood of innocent Jewish victims. Equally destructive in its effects was the Crusaders' view of the infidels. During the late Middle Ages it became even more important to fight the heretic closer to home in Western Europe and in

England than to destroy the nonbeliever who lived near some distant eastern sea.[4]

In England the tide began to turn against the Jews by 1189, when, at the coronation of Richard I, a series of misunderstandings resulted in fires and pillage. The mob raged through the Jewish residential area; it murdered and plundered along the way. It then became standard practice, from the end of the twelfth century and throughout the thirteenth, to impose immense fines on a variety of pretexts upon different Jewish communities. If the impositions could not be paid, the communities were then physically destroyed. There were horrible anti-Jewish massacres at Lynn, Bury St. Edmonds, Lincoln, Norwich, Stamford, and York. In 1219 King John imprisoned all the Jews of the realm until he extorted 66,000 marks from them. In keeping with such a policy, the king and his ministers refused to submit to those ecclesiastical rules which would have transferred economic activities from the secular to the church courts. The Royal Exchequer was not about to relinquish its control over any aspect of Jewish finance.[5]

The material position of the Jews in England grew worse both in the years of the twelfth-century Renaissance, when fresh winds of inquiry in the intellectual world, themselves the outpourings of Arab and Jewish philosophers, were bringing new ways of viewing the cosmos, God, and humanity,[6] and in the thirteenth century, when a reinvigorated Papal orthodoxy helped to hasten the expulsion of the Jews from England. The Church drew up a whole series of humiliating proscriptions against the Jews, which among other requirements made conversion sermons obligatory for them to hear, introduced the yellow badge of shame, and forbade all social relations between Christians and Jews.[7] During this period, when the Franciscan Friars reached England, their zeal for conversion and their religious fanaticism against the Jews were added to the popular conception that Jewish usurers were growing rich at the expense of the peasantry. We recall that in Chaucer's *Prioresses Tale*, the Jews were

> Sustened by a lord . . .
> For foule usure and lucre of vilenye.[8]

Obviously the Prioress knew, as the common people did not, that ultimately the king, and sometimes even the leaders of the local churches profited from Jewish moneylending.[9] As for Jews themselves, because technically they were Crown property, they were unable to claim their own possessions; the loans of any Jew belonged to his lord. Between 1239 and 1249 almost one-fifth of the entire royal revenue was derived from fines imposed on English Jewry.[10] By the end of the thirteen century such a practice had progressively not only impoverished the Jews, but, combined with more stringent codes of anti-Jewish legislation including the extension against usury, also paved the way for the 1290 expulsion. Deprived now of the one means of livelihood formerly accorded them, usury; prevented by the monopolistic practices of the medieval guilds from venturing into manufacture and trade; and unsuited for farming on the basis of temporary land-purchasing powers granted to them, the Jews were no longer needed in England. Moreover, at this time the king had access to Christian moneylenders from Lombardy and from Cahiers, the Cahorsins. With the blessings of the Church, these were able to practice usury through a legal fiction. After having imposed a huge fine upon them as his final gesture, Edward I then officially banished all his Jews from England.[11]

Despite all this, one should remember that not every moment of Jewish life in the Middle Ages was one of unrelieved gloom. The Anglo-Jewish community from the days of William the Conqueror until its banishment in 1290, and to a lesser extent even during its informal sojourn in the Elizabethan and Cromwellian periods, maintained its own civic, judicial, financial, religious, social, and cultural institutions. Not all Jews were financiers who, for their own good or ill, sustained the English monarchs. By now it is conceded that Jews were found in the army and among weapons manufacturers, and a few, in isolated settlements, were even engaged in agriculture. Sometimes moneylenders were also silversmiths, jewelers, and artisans. The Jews had poets, philosophers, and physicians in their midst. It has been suggested that some Jews had close personal and business relations with Christian intellectuals at Oxford and Cambridge. England was home in the thirteenth century for a leading Talmudist, Elijah Menahem of London. During these years English Jewry produced able translations of the Hebrew liturgy into English. Culturally, there was a far greater rate of literacy among the Jews than there was in the general community.[12]

Though Geoffrey Chaucer wrote *The Canterbury Tales* almost a century after the Jews had been banished from the country, this magnum opus of his later years carries on the tradition of the Jews' devilish associations. In it there are scattered references to those who "blaspheme treacherously," "worse than the Jews," who by so doing mutilate Christ's body anew.[13] But its most glaring example is the blood-libel story, told by one of the pilgrims, the Lady Prioress, on the way to the shrine of St. Thomas à Becket, at Canterbury.

How shall we account for Chaucer's decision to include a tale of ritual murder as one of the anecdotes to entertain a traveling group of pilgrims? It is by now generally accepted that Chaucer personally knew no Jews. But Chaucer himself was a member of a courtly circle, and was a well-traveled man. As a diplomat and negotiator of commercial and peace treaties he must have acquired a cosmopolitan outlook. At first glance it would seem that such an attitude would hardly be in keeping with the sentiments concerning Jews offered up in the name of piety by a Lady Prioress. Perhaps

Chaucer himself may have wondered how genuine her piety really was. How could he then have selected the story of an atrocity commonly attributed to the Jews as the legend most supportive of the Virgin's miraculous powers?

In enlarging upon that seeming paradox, critics make the mistake of judging Chaucer by present-day standards. They compound their error by affirming Chaucer's characters to be real in the modern, or journalistic sense.[14] If his pilgrims were then credible, or lifelike as contemporary literary creations are, then either (a) the Prioress's piety is sufficient to mute the more loathsome aspects of her tale—how the child was murdered by the Jews because of their hatred for Christians and Christianity—or how the Jews themselves were brutally punished for their ghastly deed, or (b) Chaucer intends the sarcasm he attributes to the Prioress's personality to extend to the *Tale* itself. In this sense then Chaucer would become a modern satirist, eager not only to amuse by the power of his wit, but also to reform through the art of gentle, and sometimes not-so-gentle, caricature.

These arguments sound spurious. Chaucer was primarily a man of his age.[15] It would be misreading the tenor of his times to argue that his cosmopolitanism, or his acquaintance with French and Italian culture, would have helped shape a mental attitude hardly in keeping with the vicious sentiments concerning Jews that were spoken in the name of selfless devotion by a Lady Prioress. The twelfth-century Renaissance was characterized not only by a vast expanse and breadth of knowledge, but also by an intensification of anti-Semitism in all of its ramifications. There is indeed no need to belabor the point that culture and civilization are not safeguards against prejudice of any sort. But Chaucer's enormous store of learning is further evidence of his ability to fashion characters in depth. Their subtleties, however, ought not to be thought of as testimonials to Chaucer's ability to see beyond the bigotries of his era.

The real meaning, therefore, of Chaucer's artistic process

is that it merely hints at the forward-looking nature of his creative talent. He has come close to shaping his characters in the modern sense, so that for contemporary readers they take on human qualities. But this does not tell the entire story. More important, Chaucer's method of fashioning his literary creations involved a medieval comprehension of the nature of their existence. Chaucer's pilgrims live on different levels of reality. Not only does each one of them inhabit a different universe of discourse — the Knight's world is totally different from the Miller's—but in every one of his protagonists there are correspondences between the real and the ideal. Chaucer's artistry is then revealed either in the juxtaposition of the perfect and the imperfect in each of the pilgrims on the way to Canterbury, or in their own inability to reconcile the discrepancies between the two planes of living — the spiritual and the physical.[16]

Of the various orders of the clergy called forth by Chaucer for the journey, the Monk appeared to be the wealthiest. Though presumably bound to poverty, chastity, and obedience, he loved sports, enjoyed gourmet food, had little use for learning, and was a clever businessman. "Full fat as a lord" was he; his bald pate shone as though it were "glass." There was a love-knot at the tip of the pin with which his richly furred hood was clasped and he had eyes that glowed like a fire from a furnace. Clearly, such a monk would have no part of the monastic virtues; for asceticism and self-humiliation he substituted arrogance, indulgence, and pleasure, which he derived from a variety of sources—from hunting, an activity expressly forbidden as a cruel pastime by the Church, from incomes accruing to the monastery in lands and rents (and from confiscating the payments on debts due usurers[17]), and from a fondness for rich foods and good company. Chaucer understood his Monk but he did not like him, so that all of the Monk's unchurchly attitudes found their expression in *The Shipman's Tale*. Chaucer must have thought even less of the Friar, whose effective license for begging put into practice his natural penchant for greediness, while it advanced his tendency to lechery with the women. If the author laughingly stamped his Friar as a "worthy limitour" because his begging had the blessings of the Church, he had even less use for that factotum of the ecclesiastical court, the Summoner, who, by practicing blackmail and extortion, promised poor townsmen and villagers either to reduce to to cancel the cost of their fines in court. Chaucer found that other rogue, the Pardoner, who had taken Holy Orders, beneath contempt. The Pardoner would make rounds on the different parishes to collect funds from simple sinners in return for their absolution through contact with relics blessed in Rome. He gulled the naive into believing that he was shriving their souls with his displays of "pigges bones," or a bejeweled cross, or of a piece of the sail of the boat from which St. Peter was alleged to have fished in Lake Tiberius, in Galilee. So successful was he, Chaucer observed, that his financial returns averaged more in one day than what the honest toiling parson achieved in two whole months.[18] The Pardoner's effrontery knew no bounds; in his introduction to his own *Tale*, designed to show that love of money is the root of all evil, he told the members of the pilgrimage what an effective practitioner of avarice he himself was. No more adept charlatan than he could have ended his narrative with a call to the Host, as the worst sinner of them all, to step forward and receive absolution.[19]

Such disassociations between author and character simply do not turn Chaucer's irony into a modernist account. He is not to be regarded as an active reformer flaying the Church for its sins. If he mocked his clerics, it was because he saw the width of the gap between the ideals they mouthed and their behavior. But he was not an activist in the contemporary sense. His trenchant observations on how the clergy tricked the lay people of his times were no rallying cries for reform. Nor did the acerbity with which he detailed any clerical traffic in ill-gotten wealth extend to the Lady Prioress. For all that he teased her ever so mildly, he was quite taken with her devotion, her piety, her "gentilesse."

His Prioress became for him the symbol of Marian worship. Legends of the miraculous powers of the Virgin multiplied during the twelfth century. The supernatural wonders attributed to her became staples of common religious thought. The tale the Prioress would tell would further identify her as a follower of the Virgin, whose devotee she was. As one who was herself dedicated to maintaining the shrines of martyred saints, she had joined a company on the way to Canterbury. What better example could she give of her religious devotion than to relate the story of a boy martyr, later sainted because he was done to death by the Jews?

Chaucer tells us that the Prioress, as the administrator of a nunnery, attended on the pilgrimage by her entourage of a nun and a priest, had all the habits of a gentlewoman. Her table manners were perfect, no morsel of food ever dropped untowardly from her lips. Her niceties of deportment extended to her character.

> And sikerly she was of greet desport
> And ful plesaunt and amyable of port,
> And peyned hire to countrefete cheere
> Of court, and to been estâtlich of manere,
> And to ben holden digne of reverence.

Physically, she typified the ideal medieval beauty; she possessed a high forehead, almost a span wide, slate-grey eyes, a white skin, and a rosebud mouth. While her French might not have passed muster with royalty—she had never been to Paris—it was nevertheless commendable. All in all, hers were the courtly virtues. She was so tenderhearted that she could not abide more than a mild oath. She used her napkin with finesse. Her devotion to her little dogs, whom she had with her at all times, was the very essence of kindliness; she would feed them roast meat, milk, and fine breads and wept to see any animal, even a mouse, mistreated.

She wore a bejeweled rosary from which a golden brooch was suspended, inscribed with the legend *Amor Vincit Omnia* (Love Conquers All).[20]

Nominally, such attributes as her "tendre herte," her mild "ooth...but by Seinte Loy," her love of animals, her ladylike decorum, her gentility and civility (we recall how even the rude Host was humbled by her presence) proclaimed an ideal woman given over to piety. But in their eagerness to view the Lady Prioress as the product of a modern chracterization, some students of Chaucer have embarked on two opposite paths. Either they load Chaucer's lighthearted mockery of the Nun with a sense of satire beyond its probable intent, or they embellish her religious feelings beyond credibility. In the first group there are those who emphasize the stereotypical nature of her medieval beauty as proof of Chaucer's blatant indictment against all the worldly pleasures and materialism to which the Church was prone. Here the argument runs that her misplaced love of animals was another example of the sacrilegious nature of her activities. Animals were not supposed to accompany clerics on their peregrinations about the countryside. Her concern for feeding her pets delicacies of white meat soaked in milk, when the poor of the parishes all over England were starving, would then provide additional evidence of Chaucer's disenchantment with the Church. What, after all, did it matter that the Prioress was capable of possessing that good taste demonstrated by people of high estate? Plainly, her imitative mannerisms, her French that almost but not quite passed muster at court, her wrongly weighted charities, her little affectations, possibly symbolized by the ambiguous insignia she wore, and the physical perfection of her beauty all proclaimed her to be what she was not. Indeed, there were stories of medieval nuns in those days that frequently recounted how they exceeded the rules of their orders by traveling abroad unwarrantedly. Disregarding the need for seclusion, these nuns engaged in large business ventures and frequently winked at their vows of modesty, humility, and chastity. As administrators of large priories, they may, in addition, have treated some of their subordinates cruelly, or have shown blatant favoritism to others. Thus the case is made that while the Lady Prioress was worldly, her sentimental tale contrasted with her character.[21] Still others, who marvel at the *Tale*, would then allow that the Lady Nun reveled in the purity of the child's heart; his murder evoked in her a sense of thwarted motherhood. She therefore told her story with an air of sweet innocence and must have regarded it as an extension of the "range of human experience."[22]

Perhaps the truth about Chaucer's Nun lies between these two extremes. Obviously, she had no business gadding about the countryside when she should have been attending to the business of her Order. Certainly, the off-color stories and obscene comments indulged in by some of the pilgrims would not be fit material for a Lady Nun to hear. Much has also been made of the fact that she declared herself love's servant. But was she bound to the spirit or to the flesh?[23] Simply put, it could be that all her follies stemmed from her "gentilesse." This might well have been Chaucer's way of indicating how most nuns who rose to executive positions aspired to more noble status. At its very worst, the Prioress's improper behavior was still on the fringe of that complex of worldly living which Chaucer deplored in the other churchmen. Hers was not the materialism of the Monk, the lechery of the Friar, the extortionist practice of the Summoner, the avariciousness of the Pardoner. It is by now well know that the Church in Chaucer's day had grown rich with legacies and endowments presented to it by the nobility and upper classes. Ecclesiastical courts, with their jurisdiction over inheritances, over the institution of marriage, and over matters of individual religious transgressions, also acquired enormous power. But Chaucer plainly did not intend to hold his Prioress up as the living prototype for all that was wrong with the medieval Church. Instead, he was intent upon fashioning a medieval nun, some of whose secular failing belied her ideals of churchly perfection.

And because she was of her own age and time, her deep-seated racial bigotry and anti-Semitic hatred did not, in the context of her personality, deflect from her religious devotion. In this sense the Lady escaped Chaucer's scorn. Concerns then over her worldliness or her otherworldliness, her frustrated maternal instincts, and her royal ways,[24] which are not quite up to par, become irrelevant in the light of her story.

As early as the fifth century of the Common Era, Christians had accused Jews of murdering Christian children in order to use their blood for religious purposes. These legends were natural extensions of such stock themes as that the Jews were the devil's emissaries, or that they would murder a child to uphold their religious beliefs. In the Prioress's mind, the Jews had conspired to kill the boy because Satan dwelled in their hearts and because the little boy's worship of the Virgin, the song he sang to her, flouted the laws of Judaism. Plainly, the Prioress had based her view on certain early Christian religious superstitions. Simple Christian folk had long ago observed that Jews would prepare a reddish mixture of nuts, wine, and apples to be offered at the Passover Meal as symbolic of the mortar used by the Israelites in Egypt. That food was mistaken for blood, despite the taboos in Judaism against the use of blood. By the same process of transferral, any reddish, moldy deposit on a communion wafer was regarded as a desecration of the Host, a charge that was then imputed to the Jews. Because they were capable of mutilating Christ's body, as seen symbolically in changes in the wafer, could they not equally be guilty of murdering Christian children for secret ritual purposes? An even more fearful association was deduced from the practice recorded in ancient Israel that the ritual of the Passover sacrifice required that the blood of the animal be spilled on the altar. And as Christ symbolized the supreme sacrifice, so too could the blood of innocent Christian children have been required by the Jews.[25]

The story reappeared in England in 1144, where Theobald of Cambridge, a converted Jew who had become a monk, accused the Jews of Norwich of murdering a boy named William. The myth was repeated in Gloucester (1168), Bristol (1183), Bury St. Edmonds (1186), and then in London. There, in 1244, certain converted Jews, living in a house called the *Domus Conversum*, an institution maintained by the Jewish community under duress, declared that they had seen devilish inscriptions carved into the body of a dead child. After the remains had been exhumed and the writings studied, these were deemed sufficient proof that the youngster had been killed by Jews for ritual reasons. The whole affair gave King Henry III an excuse to impose a fine of 60,000 marks upon the entire community. But the most famous of all English boy martyrs was Hugh of Lincoln, presumably murdered by the Jews in 1255 after a representative council of English Jewry had deliberated upon the deed. One Jew, near whose home the body was found, confessed under torture, and implicated his coreligionists. One hundred Jews were arrested; eighteen of them were hanged immediately when they demanded that their trials be held before a mixed jury of Christians and Jews. The remaining eighty-two were sentenced and convicted, but were released from prison at the request of Richard of Cornwall, to whom all the Jews of the kingdom had earlier been mortgaged. He was concerned that his property be protected. But little Hugh of Lincoln, who may accidentally have fallen into a pit while playing, was buried with full funeral honors. Later, he was sainted and canonized. His grave became a shrine until the time of the Reformation.[26]

The story that the Prioress told repeats many of these earlier particulars attributed to Hugh of Lincoln. Her *Tale* was set in a "far countree," in Asia. There, in a certain city where the Jews practiced usury, a little "clergeoun," a seven-year-old student, who had just learned how to read, was eager to sing the praises of the Virgin Mary. He would walk through the Jewish section of the town and repeat the *Alma Redemptoris*, a hymm of praise to Mary, which he now knew by rote, having listened to the older pupils. But the Jews grew so angry with the child when they heard him sing, that they engaged a murderer to way lay him and slit his throat. After the foul deed, the assassin cast the child's body into a pit. Later, when his mother sought him, she heard his voice issuing from the cesspool where he had been thrown. Thereupon, a magistrate who was called to the town decreed that the Jews be tortured one at a time for their crime and then be executed. This was done, and the townspeople then laid the child's body upon a bier in the church. But his singing would not cease. Miraculously, the dead boy then informed the Abbot of the monastery that the Virgin Mary had promised to take the child to heaven, if the grain she had placed on his tongue was removed. For that alone enabled him to sing. Once the grain was lifted, the child was silenced. The townspeople buried him in a marble tomb amidst full funeral honors. The story, the Prioress admitted, was remarkably like that of Hugh of Lincoln for whom the Jews had decreed a similar fate.

This last reference to Hugh of Lincoln also united the Prioress with the Virgin Mary, while it tightened the bond between the blood-libel accusation and the Virgin's intervention on behalf of the martyred children. In many of these miracle stories that intervention sometimes took another form: the Virgin restored the child to life. But it would have been in keeping with the characterization of a medieval nun to have her boy martyr enjoy the rewards of heaven. A less dramatic change, but more significant in its effect, was Chaucer's decision to allow the boy to become a chorister, rather than remain the student he was in other legends. Not only would his singing have further infuriated the Jews, but would have heightened the poignancy of the miracle itself. His singing had, in effect, continued beyond the grave.

In real life, however, the Hugh of Lincoln tale merely

signaled a whole series of similar accusations that would revive with particular vehemence in 1276 and 1279, and would be woven into an ever more virulent fabric of progressively intensive anti-Jewish proscriptions.[28]

The story of the boy martyrs then entered into the English ballad tradition. Circulated among country folk, these legends were called "Sir Hugh," "The Jew's Daughter," and "Sir Hugh or The Jew's Daughter." They even crossed the ocean to America.[29]

Several evaluations of the Prioress's version skirt the anti-Semitic charge inherent in the miracle story. As in her description, so too here, the emphasis is on the ideal nun who emerges as the teller of the tale. Though she herself spares no words with reference to the malice of the Jews, or to the frightfulness of their punishment, it is as though readers would want her feminine charms to obviate the horror of the story. In fact, critical commentary has united to such a degree on the sweetness of her delivery that the more repulsive features of her story tend to be lost sight of. It is even contended that the tale's ugly qualities are diminished because of its foreign setting and by virtue of its explanatory note concerning the Jews' preoccupation with usury. To set it all to rights, there is also the theory that here in *The Prioresses Tale,* "naturalism and the supernatural make peace in miracle."[30] Such opinions avoid the shrillness of the deed. At best they serve as overpowering testimonies to Chaucer's success in shaping his Lady Prioress. Readers, having duly considered her charms and her faults, manage to extract from her story of ritual murder only the piety it reveals.

However, one recent interpretation of the Prioress and her *Tale* would weigh Chaucer's sarcasm in his treatment of the Prioress's personality—her coyness, her "attractiveness in the mode of the medieval romance with all its worldliness," the ambiguous motto on her brooch—against her piety, and find the latter wanting. But having declared the inadequacy of her faith, such an interpretation would then regard her story as Chaucer's "implicit condemnation" of the ritual-murder charge. Further proof for this point of view is the writer's certainty that the courtly audience for whom Chaucer wrote would recognize the distinction between the Nun's bigotry and her seeming devotion, and would, therefore, regard her tale with derision.[31] Yet this courtly audience, removed more or less one hundred years from real Jews in time, were the descendants of those barons and lesser nobility who were in the forefront of instigations against the Jews. Of course, there were always well-meaning Christians, both clergy and lay people, who protected Jews in times of massacres. In addition, many Popes frequently deplored the ritual-murder stories,[32] but such modifications did not alter the basically anti-Semitic patterns that emerged during the latter half of the twelfth century in England and grew in intensity throughout the succeeding hundred years.[33]

Only the Parson in *The Canterbury Tales* was prepared to extend a sense of Christian love to sinners. But in the Middle Ages no such compassion would ever have been intended for nonbelievers. Indeed, it would be idle to argue that the Parson's attitude was but a reflection of Chaucer's feelings toward heretics. He did not choose that variant of the blood-libel legend where the child was restored to life and the Jews converted.[34] To hazard what prompted Chaucer's selection of a particularly bloody and cruel ritual-murder story as most supportive of the Virgin's power would be foolhardy. What is certain, however, is that in making sure that the child received the rewards of Heaven, Chaucer reaffirmed a staple of medieval thought. That the Jews died was therefore of no account. According to medieval standards, this was their just retribution.

Looked at from another angle, blood-libel accusations were intrinsic to the maintenance of anti-Semitic impulses, while at the same time churches benefited financially from the immediate results of such miracle stories. Since shrines multiplied wherever the miracles of the boy martyrs occurred, local clergy were not at all averse to the ritual-murder charges. On occasion they even helped foment them.³⁵ Chaucer, aware of the economic privileges accruing to such parishes by the repetition of these miracles, might then have cast his Prioress's lot in with such clergy.

Chaucer's Nun, we recall, was credible and lifelike, full of contradictions, perplexities, an ambiguous personality, so that the difficulties encountered in assessing her characterization make for quick mislabeling. She is called real, or modern, in the journalistic sense, when in truth, as a medieval figure she moved on different levels of reality ascribed to her. On one of them, as the ideal medieval Nun, she reflected that religious piety which was part of her available stock in trade, which, in the aggregate, was also fed by her hatred of the Jews.

Precisely because she lived in a hierarchical society, in which the scale of values attached to medieval romances—chivalry, love of truth, justice, loyalty, and purity of heart—were transferred from the secular realm to the religious, she was able to use similar measuring rods for her story. And because in such a scheme the Jews were always the alien factor, she regarded them as villains. Had Chaucer enlarged his Nun to grant her the capacity to understand human suffering, she would not, as a character, have fulfilled the role demanded of her by her story. Therefore, her attitude toward the Jews was as much a part of her as the Pardoner's bag of tricks belonged to him. That Chaucer saw fit to laugh at the relics, but was in deadly earnest about the Jews in *The Prioresses Tale,* may simply be the result of his knowing pardoners in the flesh. What he knew of Jews as human beings remains problematical.

What is know, however, is that unsubstantiated charges of ritual murder have continued to plague the Jews well into the twentieth century. Tragically, these blood libels have led to untold suffering, to the torture and execution of hundreds of Jews, and to the despoliation of their properties and their communities.³⁶

2
Venice and Belmont

MANY aspects of existence in the Middle Ages yielded to the Renaissance. Serfs became workers; towns and cities arose. The burgeoning middle and merchant classes at last received proper recognition. Revised codes of civil and criminal law, the development of Parliament, classroom instruction conducted in English, and a broadening sense of nationalism—all these factors made Shakespeare's world very different from Chaucer's. Yet the anti-Semitism of Shakespeare's day exhibited the same stereotypical patterns as the earlier blood-libel legends. This was so because the handful of converted Jews in Chaucer's London, and the thirty-seven householders of Jewish origin, two hundred years later in Tudor England,[1] were too few in number to effect any appreciable changes in Christian attitudes toward them. At best, there must have been only a handful of Jews in the Elizabethan period. Otherwise how can it be that out of a total of fifteen hundred plays, only a scant nine bore any reference to Jews?[2] And this situation prevailed at a time when the drama was the most popular form of entertainment. Therefore, in the late sixteenth century, when a set of historic circumstances generated a renewed flurry of anti-Semitic agitation, these merely repeated the patterns of prejudice drawn earlier in the Middle Ages. If the Jews in *The Prioresses Tale* were the devil's cohorts, so too did they remain for many more years than the two centuries that elapsed between the Hugh of Lincoln incident, rewoven into Chaucerian *rime royal*, and the two significant dramas dealing with Jews in the Elizabethan period, *The Jew of Malta* and *The Merchant of Venice*.

Despite an official ban against their presence in Elizabethan England, there were both small communities of crypto-Jews, or Marranos, who had escaped the clutches of the Spanish Inquisition, and small groups of professing members of the faith. A sister to two prominent Marrano merchants in London's community of New Christians was Sara Ames; one of her nephews served as an intelligence agent in the Azores for Sir Francis Drake. More important, she was the wife of Dr. Roderigo Lopez, a Portuguese Marrano physician, who, as a member of the British College of Physicians, delivered lectures on anatomy. He was also a medical consultant to Queen Elizabeth and to the Earl of Essex. It was Lopez's misfortune that he was related by marriage to an ex-Marrano, Alvaro Mendes, a Jewish adviser to the Turkish Sultan, who at that time was eager to cement an Anglo-Turkish alliance against Spain. In the process, Lopez hoped to secure British approval of the rights of the Pretender to the Portuguese throne, Don Antonio, the prior of Crato, who was himself of Jewish origin. But the scheme backfired, for after Drake failed in his expedition against Portugal in 1589, Lopez transferred his allegiance to Spain. This antagonized the powerful Earl of Essex, stepson to the Earl of Leicester, who had inherited Lopez's services. Since Essex was now all for war against Spain, he and his party provided evidence, which may well have been false, that Lopez had conspired with Spain to poison the Queen. Though Lopez was defended by Lord Cecil in court and the Queen herself had doubts as to his guilt, he was convicted and hanged at Tyburn in June 1594.[3] Records recount that he confessed to everything so that he would be spared racking before execution, and there is a possible reference to Lopez in *The Merchant of Venice*, where Bassanio protests his suffering love for Portia by saying that he "lives upon the rack." She responds by urging him to confess

> What treason there is mingled with your love.
> (3.2.28)

for she fears that he may well

> . . . speake upon the racke
> Where men enforced doe speake anything.
> (3.2.34-35)[4]

This time the irony was compounded, not in the play, for Bassanio did not need the rack to confess his true love for Portia, but in real life. To the derisive laughter of the mob, Lopez died, confessing his love for Jesus Christ. But the crowd, witnessing his hanging, may not have known that Lopez acted as a secret agent to dispatch funds for the maintenance of a synagogue in Antwerp, or that genuine Jewish religious services were held in the home of one of Lopez's associates.[5]

Between the time of Lopez's sentence and his execution, Christopher Marlowe's play *The Jew of Malta* was the rage of the London theatrical season. Its source is unknown. Perhaps Marlowe, with his penchant for power, fashioned his Barabas, the Jew of Malta, after Joseph Nasi, Duke of Naxos, predecessor to Alvaro Mendes, and himself an adviser to the Turkish Sultan. However, the Duke of Naxos was as philanthropic as Barabas was miserly. Such an analogy would have to be discounted on that score alone. What was more important was that as a result of the diplomatic intrigue attributed to Lopez, the Jew had become a popular topic in courtly and intellectual circles. Marlowe's literary comprehension of him as an unprincipled Machiavellian hero fitted in nicely with the notion of the ubiquitous, villainous Jew driven by a lust for wealth to practice diplomatic skullduggery. Of course, like his medieval ancestors on the stage, Barabas still bore the marks of the devil. Treading about the hidden springs of the play, he is forever busying himself with poisoning wells, orphaning children, and rejoicing in villainy. Having taken an additional Renaissance cue from the Florentine, Barabas, before his fated end, is yet able to revel in his riches, to persist in his gruesome activities, and to engage in foreign diplomacy. Through a series of ruses, Barabas, as a caricature of a merchant prince, not only regains his confiscated wealth, but manages to wreak his vengeance on all those about him, on his converted daughter, Abigail, upon the two rivals for her hand, and against two monks who have heard of his unspeakable crimes. He also effectively eliminates a whore and a thief who were out to fleece him of his wealth. He even becomes Governor of Malta, but his last ploy, to destroy the Turkish army of occupation, signals his own demise. He falls into a boiling cauldron intended originally for his enemies.[6]

Marlowe's style was pure Elizabethan theater, with lots of crude action, bombast, high-flown rhetoric, and sweeping blank verse. The audience loved it all the more because it catered to its taste to see the clever Jew undone and his Italianate bag of tricks explode.

Nothing about Barabas encompassed that meaningful villainy which was to become Shylock's in *The Merchant of Venice*. Barabas was quite content to have his daughter, Abigail, enter a nunnery so she could trap his hated Christians. The instructions with which Barabas would better the deeds of his Christian clients spelled simple vengeance. But Shylock's demands for justice arose from a more complicated motivation. At the same time, Shylock's relationship to Jessica introduced new ideas and attitudes concerning intra-Jewish relationships, material that had never before been so adroitly handled by English dramatists.

But comparisons between Barabas and Shylock have been legion. Long ago, the influence of *The Jew of Malta* upon Shakespeare's *Merchant* had been carefully plotted, line for line and scene for scene.[7] Any resemblances between the two dramas would make it appear all the more likely that Shakespeare was intent on mounting a production that would improve upon *The Jew of Malta*. He could not have done better with the result. *The Merchant of Venice* proved to be a happy choice; not only did it involve two businessmen catering to the laughter of merchants in the audience, but it also benefited from the interest aroused in the Lopez case.

Shakespeare did not have to go too far afield for either the prototype of the Jew he was seeking or the story he would build around him. Avid researchers have carefully scrutinized the sources Shakespeare had available, and have discovered several that would have suited his purposes admirably. One morality play, *The Three Ladies of London*, includes a good Jewish merchant, who, though he is successful in dissuading his debtor, Mercadore of London, from converting to Mohammedanism in order to escape payment of his obligation, nevertheless remains a Jewish rogue and scoundrel. For Mercadore is happy at having been able to cheat the "filthy Jew." Closer to *The Merchant of Venice* in theme, characterization, and action, however, were two legends popular in Elizabethan times. One was the story of the pound of flesh, and the other the matter of a suitor's choosing among three caskets. The issue of a mechant's demanding a pound of flesh should the debt become forfeit was Oriental in origin; ultimately it found its way into a collection of Italian tales, *Il Pecorone,* by Ser Giovanni Fiorentino (Milan, 1558). Here the pound-of-flesh theme is combined with the matter of wooing by means of testing, but without the caskets, though this story does include the other basic elements of *The Merchant of Venice,* even the rescue of the Christian debtor by a disguised lady in court, and the ring incident. In the *Gesta Romanorum,* a medieval collection of tales,

Shakespeare found the account of the caskets. He might also have come upon an almost intact version of *The Merchant of Venice* story in a play called *The Jew*, produced in 1579, and acted, perhaps, at the Bull Tavern. One of Shakespeare's contemporaries, Stephen Gosson, thought it represents "the greediness of worldly chusers and the bloody minds of usurers."[8]

It should be remembered that the Renaissance Venice one meets with at the very opening of the play is not only the Venice of Shylock, but also that of Antonio, Bassanio, and their friends. London merchants who were quite accustomed to charging twelve percent interest on their loans would have howled with laughter over the carryings on of an Italian merchant adventurer who lent money gratis and, indulging the fancy of some foolish friend, prepared "to send good money after bad."[9] If Bassanio, to the delight of the London crowd, was in reality a fortune hunter like Jason, (for Portia's "sunny locks" signified *his* "golden fleece") and if Antonio was a careless merchant, why not enter into a bond of a pound of flesh as a "merrie sporte?" For those with a precise yearning for historic truth, mutilation as a way of sealing a covenant between debtor and lender had indeed been an ancient practice in the classical world, deriving originally from the Law of the Roman Twelve Tablets, but this practice had long ago been abandoned.[10]

It was not resorted to in Shakespeare's day and for this reason *The Merchant of Venice* remains a comedy. Despite the whetting of the knife in the trial scene, no blood is shed and for an Elizabethan audience Shylock's forced conversion to Christianity is no punishment. Instead it would be seen as opening avenues of grace for Shylock whose soul these many years has been pent up in his sober universe. But because the story of *The Merchant of Venice* operated within the context of the legend and its characters cannot escape from its framework, Antonio's actions must also be judged by the criteria of the wager. At the very outset of the play Antonio would accept the sporting aspect of the bet. The "merrie sporte" of a pound of flesh was too preposterous to consider. Certainly, all his ships would return. And it has also been argued that Shylock, in first proposing mutilation was not the usually devilish medieval Jew, the stock figure anticipated by Elizabethan audiences, but that once Antonio spurned his "kind offer" of 3000 ducats and no interest, then Shylock began to revert to kind. Thus, if later Shylock's loathing would force him to say

> Ile have my bond, speake not against my bond.
> (3.3.7)

so now, early on, Antonio's hatred for the Jew would make him insist upon the letter of the law of the bond. It is this twist to the old fable, that Antonio, in his cruelty, unwittingly moves the demand for a pound of flesh from a "merrie sporte" to literalness, that calls forth a series of dramatic incidents, each one mounting progressively to ever higher levels of suspense. This increasing intensity of action is due not only to the revenge in which Shylock prepared to "feed fat" upon the careless Christian, but also from Antonio's own heedless pride and arrogance.

Though he normally would neither borrow nor lend at interest, on Bassanio's behalf Antonio was prepared to negotiate with a Jewish miser. From Shylock's illustration that there was a parallel to the gains achieved by usury in the Old Testament when Jacob struck a bargain with Laban in the matter of breeding multi-streaked lambs, Antonio was only able to declare that the yield from such living kind had been "fashioned by the hand of heaven." Merchant though he was, to Antonio the very object of usury, to have "barraine mettall" breed, was unnatural. He could not understand how interest is bred from the principal, and so he asked Shylock whether he told the story of Jacob and Laban and the sheep to "make interest good?" Shylock, despairing of Antonio's ability to comprehend the biblical analogy, merely responds

> I cannot tell, I make it breede as fast.
> (1.3.100)

Despite his personal aversion to a

> divell [who] can cite Scripture for his purpose,
> (1.3.102)

Antonio's "suit" was still "moneyes." He could only respond to Shylock's outraged cry,

> Faire sir, you spet on me on Wednesday last,
> You spurn'd me on such a day; another time
> You cald me dog: and for these curtesie
> Ile lend you thus much moneyes.
> (1.3.129-32)

with

> I am as like to call thee so againe,
> To spet on thee againe, to spurne thee too.
> If thou wilt lend this money, lend it not
> As to thy friends, for when did friendship take
> A breede of barraine mettall of his friend?
> But lend it rather to thine enemie
> Who if he breake, thou maist with better face
> Exact the penalties.
> (1.3.133-40)

Here there is evidence of Antonio's inviting his own doom. Only friends lend money gratis, and as Shylock's enemy he would "face the penalty." Yet on the other hand, Shylock was willing to overlook Antonio's arrogant behavior and to forgo any interest on the loan.

> Why looke you, how you storme,
> I would be friends with you and have
>   your love,
> Forget the shames that you have staind
>   me with,
> Supplie your present wants, and take no doite
> Of usance for my moneyes; and youle not
>   heare me.
> (1.3.141-45)

Such kindness on Shylock's part (earlier he had been prepared to "feed fat the ancient grudge" he bore Antonio) in no way mitigated Antonio's stance. Nor did it diminish the heedless, unthinking cruelty of Antonio's colleagues and hangers-on. Bassanio's reaction to Shylock's offer of no interest and the pound of flesh, since the pound, after all, was not likely to fall due, was even more than Antonio's steeped in malice. "I like not faire termes and a villain's mind" (1.3.185).[11]

Bound up with this distrust was the distinction in the uses of wealth for Shylock and for the inhabitants of Belmont. Shylock was the one sour note in this merry jest where Renaissance man had the wisdom to enjoy wealth, to use it generously, if carelessly, and to insure each other's friendship through its efficacy. Shylock, however, displayed an anxiety about his wealth.[12] He knew that to insure his own success he must allow his "barren metal" to breed. Here then was that inherent irony in the uses to which riches were put. In their opulent Belmont setting, replete with chances for good fortune hidden in one of the three caskets, Portia and Bassanio saw no contradiction between their social feeling for wealth, with its relationship to their love, and the fact that, given the chance, Shylock too might have seen good purposes for his wealth. But since Shakespeare intended Shylock to be the comic villain of the piece, Shylock's relationship to his own wealth had to become mechanical, devoid of emotion, so that he confused his love for his daughter with his flown ducats. It mattered little then that the Christians' acquisition of wealth was there to confirm Bassanio's love, but it became a source of ridicule for Shylock's concern over wealth to include a seemingly disparate frame of reference, that of his love, a living daughter. Since Shylock was used to breeding a barren metal, he ought to have seen no linkage between such wealth and affection, while his Renaissance contemporaries "used the one to beget the other." It would follow then that the humor in Shylock's disjointed cries of "O my daughter, O my ducats!" became even more laughable when subjected to the cruelly obscene allusions of Salanio and Salerio to his loss.[13] But love and joy and music were the natural concomitants of the wealth stolen from Shylock to which Jessica and Lorenzo fell heir.

There is no evidence from *The Merchant of Venice* that Shakespeare knew anything of Jewish family life, much less of the strong ties of filial devotion that commonly existed between parents and children. But for the purposes of the play, Jessica's cruelty, faithlessness, and desertion become complementary to her lover's greed. She too, like Lorenzo, steals what is not hers, and concurs with her new-found friends in their estimate of her father.[14] In fact, all of the characters in the play, except for the Duke and Portia, excoriate Shylock for his blatant cruelty. So effective has this practice been that its cumulative impact has tricked some serious Shakespearian scholars into measuring each of Shylock's actions by the standards of a Bassanio, a Lorenzo, a Jessica, or a Gratiano, themselves imaginary creatures. Infected with the poison flowing from the attitudes of Shylock's enemies, these students of the Bard would comprehend each and every one of Shylock's actions as motivated by loathing, greed, venality, and sheer hatred for its own sake. Such scholars would deny Shylock even those moments of humanization with which his creator occasionally endowed him. For Shylock's impassioned cry, "Hath not a

Jew eyes? etc.,'' they would remind readers that it came in response to some crude observations by Salanio and Salerio on Shylock's losses, and that it ended with the Jew's cry for vengeance. "The villainy you teach me I will execute, and it shall goe hard but I will better the instruction" (3.1.66).[15]

Seen from these perspectives, *The Merchant of Venice* can be thought of as a lesson upon the uses to which a Christian and a Jew may put their material possessions, or it may be regarded as a comment upon the capricious turns in fortune to which a "merrie sport" can lead. But the most favored lens for viewing the play these many centuries is the one that focuses on the drama as an allegory. This does not mean that the action comprehended in the play is itself symbolical, but that the ideas and morality intended by that action are. That intention is the conflict of values between the old vision of life and a new. The crass, material world of Venice is pitted against the ideal land of Belmont, where riches, though available, are not reckoned. Venice bears the guilt of its new-found commercial talents, themselves a constant reproach to the ideals of the medieval church,[16] while Belmont rejoices in that grace which finds its truest expression in a community of men presided over by a woman who is the epitome of wit and mercy. There, in Belmont, the ordeal of testing, motivated as it was by Bassanio's willing surrender of self, results in happiness and harmony. In Venice, except for a legal quibble, Antonio's ordeal of testing would have resulted in death. Since it did not, and the Jew was forced to convert, *The Merchant of Venice* may be comprehended as the vindication of the new man, the new Christian, in contradistinction to the old Jew. Close reading of the way Shakespeare developed the action validates the view that he meant to affirm the victory of an idealized, Christian way of life.

At the very opening of the play, those two practically indistinguishable puppets, Salerio and Salanio, manage to evoke the free, life-pulsating, careless world of the Christian,

Venice and Belmont

Renaissance gentleman. They try to account for merchant Antonio's weariness by his concern for his argosies at sea. But his weariness was that quality of life so often associated with the Renaissance world. Such a weariness was never hedged about by real depression. In such circumstances, it was always desirable to give of one's self and one's possessions. Giving may have indeed have been the key term, for Antonio, still short of funds and despite his sadness, is yet willing to give of himself and his future to Bassanio, his impoverished friend, who gambled for gain and lost. Such a failure would count for nothing against love, trust, and mutual friendship in that romantic world. "You know me well," says Antonio, chiding Bassanio, not for his wastefulness, but for his ambiguity.

> To winde about my love with
>   circumstance,
> And out of debt you doe
>   more wrong
> In making question of my
>   uttermost
> Than if you have made waste of all
>   I have:
> Then doe but say to me what I should
>   doe
> That in your knowledge may by me
>   be done
> And I am prest unto it.
> (1.1.164-70)

In this universe of feeling, it mattered not at all to Antonio, the symbol of the perfect Renaissance man, that Bassanio placed Portia's riches ahead of his love for her. Portia was the lady "richly left in Belmont." But Antonio was so impressed with Bassanio's fair qualities that he would never have counted the cost of the venture to that enchanted land. Indeed, Portia, Bassanio, and Antonio all matched each other in their casual disregard for practicality. Their disdain for the grubby realities of life savored of boredom, assumed or authentic. Antonio, we recall, was weary. It may be that he indulged in melancholy because he disapproved of the vanities and follies of the work-a-day world. But to his hanger-on Gratiano, there is nothing profound about Antonio's attitude. It is, at best, a pose.

> There are a sort of men whose
>   visages
> . . . do a willful stillness entertaine
> With purpose to be drest in an
>   opinion
> Of wisedome, gravity, profound
>   conceit,
> As who should say, I am sir an
>   Oracle
> And when I ope my lips, let not
>   dogge barke.
> (1.1.98-104)

There was no logic behind Antonio's "want-wit" sadness, or in Portia's despondency, her weariness, as she put it. But in the ideal, new world, to be inhabited by Portia and Antonio and Bassanio, even the self-indulgences to which emotions give rise would be allowed full play. Such happy creatures may sally forth and frolic in the wealth of feeling, whether it be "want-wit" in nature or be grounded in reason. Since logic was never the component element in such a universe, even the emphasis on moderation, on civility, on a sober thoughtfulness would not be out of keeping in such concentration on human sensibility. So Bassanio, before he is about to embark for Belmont, cautions Gratiano, by now his serving man, to maintain a certain reserved deportment.

> . . . Pray thee take paine
> To allay with some cold drops of
>   modestie

> Thy skipping spirit, lest through
>   thy wilde behavior
> I be misconstered in the place
>   I go to
> And loose my hopes.
> (2.2.181-85)

In response, Gratiano assures him

> If I doe not put on a sober habit,
> . . . .
> Use all the observance of civilitie
> Like one well studied in a sad ostent
> To please his Grandam, never trust me
>   more.
> (2.2.181-94)

Bassanio, of course, did not lose his hope. His clever selection of the right casket, whether by intuition or by a hint from Portia, also enlarges on the open, perfect, happy universe of which they will be the proud possessors. Had not the character analyses of all of the suitors in which Portia and her maid Nerissa indulged shown them, with the exception of Bassanio, to have been overly ruled by one passion, one humor, to the exclusion of other qualities? But Bassanio, as "a Venetian, a scholar, and a soldier," was obviously the whole new man, the rounded personality, who, *on trust*, gave of himself and gained a world thereby. So great was his achievement, that loss of words overcame him:

> Maddam, you have bereft me of all words,
> Onely my bloud speakes to you in my vaines,
> And there is such confusion in my powers,
> As after some oration fairely spoke
> By a beloved prince, there doth appeare
> Among the buzzing pleased multitude
> Where every something, being blent
>   together

> Turnes to a wilde of nothing, save of joy
> Expresst and not expresst.
> (3.2.182-89)

Shylock and his orientation to life provided the very antithesis to such creatures who define existence in terms of mutual love and free self-offerings, who relish emotions either for a reason or for no reason at all, who delude themselves into equating sagacity with a thoughtful demeanor, a sober cast of mind, and who pay homage to the new man who has become a miraculous composite of all the virtues. Shylock's entrance in the play has shattered this open world. His sound business principles, his musings on the amount of the loan involved, and on the grudge he bears the Christians for their hatred to his race, his clever, rabbinical analyses on usury beyond Antonio's understandings—all these break the spell of Belmont. How can an Antonio, prepared to stake all for a friend, possibly comprehend the reckonings in the mind of a moneylender, who, considering the stipulation of "three thousand ducats for three months and Antonio bound," weighs the changes of repayment for his loan? Shylock admits that he believes Antonio is a "good man," and realizes that Antonio is "sufficient"—that is, he will pay up. But in Shylock's mind,

> Ships are but boards, Saylors but men, there be land rats and water rats, water thieves, and land thieves, I meane pyrats; and then there is the perrill of waters, windes, and rocks. (1.3.22-25)

Though Shylock has nevertheless agreed to the loan, such a close accounting could only have grated on the mind of an Italian merchant moved by love never to count the cost. If, as the new man, Antonio is heedless, he may well yet enter into the forfeiture of a pound of flesh, should his "ships miscarry" and his "loan fall due." For if caution and discretion marked Shylock, carelessness and overabundant sympathy were the watchwords for Antonio'a course in life, a course in which his friends concurred.

There are other aspects to Shylock's prudent, sober world that also threaten the open, happy, loving universe of discourse that was Antonio's and his colleagues'. Shylock's dark, pent-up living may be symbolized by his house, whose windows, he warns his daughter Jessica, should be shut against the frivolous carousings and merriment of those young, masked Christian revelers. Such a silent dwelling somehow stands as a rebuke and a warning to Antonio that when the final day of reckoning does arrive, there will be no reveling for him. For Jessica, such silence, oddly enough, spells hell, but hell here is defined as tedium, or boredom, not as an unholy, ongoing, active manifestation of pain and evil. What was hell then to Jessica, the tediousness and quiet sobriety of her father's house, she managed to abandon with such callousness that even Gratiano observes

> Now, by my hood, a gentle [Gentile]
>   and no Jew!
> (2.6.58)

When that stillness in Shylock's universe is broken, it resembles a howling wilderness. Though he delighted in Antonio's misfortune at sea, Shylock shrieks at the loss of his daughter and his ducats. To an Elizabethan audience, his seeming inability to distinguish between his loss and his victory provided moments of high comedy. There was humor both in the unequal juxtaposition of the sounds, "O my daughter, O my ducats," and in his mechanical alterations between joy and sorrow.[17] Yet his daughter had deserted her faith. Shylock is not so much the miser but that he would gladly have had his Jessica "hearsed" at his feet and his ducats in her coffin. In the midst of his clowning, the Jewish moneylender grows in stature by virtue of his adversity.

At other moments in the play, when the derision is still

there but some of the humor has abated, Shylock's voice would come, to quote a famous critic, "rasping into the play like a file . . . used to sawing . . . short phrases, niggardly, ugly, curt."[18] The ugliness is compounded when Shylock makes short shrift of what could have been the loveliest of sounds, music. When he wants Jessica to keep the casements of his house locked up, it is so that she may not

> heare the drum
> And the vile squeaking of the wry-neckt Fife
> (2.5.31-32)

that belong to the merrymakers. Later, in an attempt to illustrate capriciousness, Shylock again resorts to music. But if the sounds he associates with music evoked negative connotations in his admonition to Jessica, they now are obscene in their allusions.

> You'l aske me why I rather
>   choose to have
> A weight of carrion flesh
>   than to receive
> Three thousand Ducats. Ile not
>   answer that;
> But say it is my humor. . . .
>   . . . .
> Some men there are. . .
>   . . . .
> And others, when the bagpipe
>   sings i'th nose
> Cannot contain their Urine. . .
> . . .Now for your answer;
> As there is no firme reason to be
>   rendered
> Why he cannot abide a gaping Pigge?
> Why he. . .
> Why he a woollen bagpipe; but of force
> Must yield to inevitable shame
> As to offend himselfe being offended
> So I can give no reason . . .

More than a lodged hate. . .
I beare Antonio. . . .
(4.1.57-65)

When such loathing no longer sufficed, when his mounting fury no longer sustained him, then Shylock was prepared to lapse into silence. It is symbolic of his shuttered universe that he would have his bond.

> . . . and therefore speak no more
> . . . .
> . . . .
> I'll have no speaking; I will
>   have my bond.
> (3.3.15-20)

Such silence, such stillness was alien to Belmont. Its still tenuous ties with mortality forbade it from hearing the divine harmony of the spheres,[19] yet it was continuously bathed in audible music. Portia's lines and the world she represents are odes to the power of music, which, true to its medieval heritage, is the symbol of order and perfection in the universe. It was in the rarefied air of a Renaissance Belmont that Bassanio, in the matter of the caskets, would stake his future to the accompaniment of music, as though music itself were sufficient proof that all would go well. Were he to fail, then the comfort of his beloved's tears would be his deathbed, but if success should grace his effort, then music is

> Even as the flourish, when true
>   subjects bowe
> To a new crowned Monarch; Such
>   it is
> As are those dulcet sounds in
>   breake of day
> That creep into the dreaming bridegroom's ear
> And summon him to marriage.
> (3.2.51-56)

When, however, stillness does prevail in Portia's fairyland, it is born of a comprehension that surpasses understanding. Bassanio, we recall, is speechless with the ecstasy of his love. In that last magnificent scene in Belmont, with Shylock's world destroyed, the sound not heard by human ears, the stillness, becomes the heavenly music of the spheres.

> . . . Look how the floor of heaven
> Is thick inlayed with pattens
>   of bright gold.
> There's not the smallest orbe which
>   thou beholdst
> But in his motion like an Angell
>   sings
> Still quiring to the young-eyed
>   Cherubins;
> Such harmonie is in immortall
>   soules;
> But whilst this muddy vesture of decay
> Doth grossly close it in, we
> cannot heare it.
> (5.1.67-74)

To the Elizabethans, such heavenly harmony was further proof of their belief in the great chain of being—the testament of God's perfect plan of order in the universe by which the lowliest creation was forever linked in degrees of ascent by physical, mental, or spiritual characteristics to the next manifestation of His handiwork, until union was made with the very angels themselves. But since these were invisible to mortal man, and because the music of the spheres was inaudible to his ears, only man's return to Paradise would make him truly perceptive, would make him see "as with a great light."[20]

Not Venice, but Belmont was the location for this ladder leading to perfection. Bassanio escaped from the wastrel, opulent world of Venice where the great chain of being was at best a man-made creation. Lorenzo and Jessica too fled from Shylock's silent yet discordant surroundings to Portia's open, singing world. Those for whom Portia's character was the archetype would see "not through a glass darkly," but directly.

Her provident or generous nature, then, justified her return to Shylock's loathsome environment, to vindicate her compassion and mercy for the symbol of the new man, Antonio. Such a Portia, tuned by fine music, honed by a rapier-like wit, would reduce an argument to its absurdity. Yet the cause she would represent was itself outrageous, for the law looks after all those contingencies which would have made Shylock's and Antonio's "merrie sporte" improbable. Shylock's trial bore no resemblance whatsoever to any legal principle ever practiced in any civilized country. No agreement that would have sanctioned the commission of a capital crime could be deemed legally valid. Second, legal contracts properly arrived at allow for no modifications of the original agreements. Therefore, Portia's plea for justice for the Jew, based as it is on rendering the exact amount of a pound of flesh, was fraudulent both in its initial premise, since it sanctioned murder, and in its legal implications, since it involved a change in terms.[21] At the very least, her request raised false hopes in Shylock and prolonged Antonio's fears that the knife would be used. She continued to dally with Antonio's fate when she took time out to quote from an ancient Venetian law decreeing the fate of an alien seeking to murder a citizen of the state. Like the proverbial goddess of Justice, Portia, too, was blind. But she was blind to righteousness. Shylock had to divest himself of all his property for the good of his converted daughter, and accept Christianity for his own benefit.

Because he tended to be acted upon by others, rather than to initiate action, Shylock's nature changed by virtue of this cruelty. In the symbolic sense, the play, then, is the crystallization of his promise to better the Christian's villainous instructions, but, in the realistic sense, the cruelty practiced upon him led to moments of his humanization. One critic has cautioned against sentimentalizing this transformation, while another has seen only the comic Shylock, even in the moment of his greatest despair, in the loss of his daughter.[22] But in the play there are three notable enlargements upon his character: when he upbraids Antonio who has come seeking a loan, when both his daughter and his fortune have been lost, and when he charges Christians with practicing slavery.

The first two occasions have already been alluded to.[23] But the third instance occurs just before Shylock himself is to be made to pay for his obstinacy. It is at this moment that he refers to the equal temptations before all men to perform acts of cruelty.

> You have among you many a purchast
>   slave
> Which like your Asses and your Dogs
>   and your Mules
> You use in abject and in slavish parts
> Because you bought them. Shall I say
>   to you
> Let them be free; marrie them to your
>   heires?
> Why sweate they under burthens? Let
>   their beds
> Be made as soft as yours; and let
>   their palates
> Be seasoned with such Viands; You will answer
> "The slaves are ours." So do I answer you,
> The pound of flesh which I demand of him
> Is dearly bought, is mine and I will
>   have it.
> (4.1.95-105)

With these lines, Shylock reveals greater insights than would appear fitting for a villain. He is not, of course, ennobled in the process; he shows no magnaminity, much less any understanding of that much-vaunted quality of mercy. But he does teach his hearers an awareness of that frightening perversity which motivates all men, Christians and Jews alike, sometimes to separate will and action from all constructive reason.

It is precisely this disassociation that ought to be borne in mind in a consideration of *The Merchant of Venice*. Reason has absolutely nothing whatsoever to do with the play. Shakespeare endowed unreal people with credible emotions; readers, therefore, are at liberty to evaluate those emotions. They ought not, however, to err in judging these feelings as valid reflections of the motivations of real people. For in the last analysis, Portia was not real, Shylock was not authentic, and the trial was a myth. So too are the implications that the law as derived from Shylock's Old Testament is devoid of mercy. Diligent scholars can cite biblical and later Rabbinic sources that completely reject the theory of "lex talionis," an eye for an eye, and expatiate on the divine attributes of grace and loving kindness, which men must imitate in their daily lives.[24] Had such a Jew as Shylock ever existed and had he been tried by a rabbinical court, his suit would have been rejected, and he would have been punished for attempted murder. But Shakespeare either did not know this, or did not care to know this. To complete his comedy, the symbol of the new man, the new way of life, and the new world of Belmont had to emerge triumphant. So great would be the victory that it would even encompass the devil. Encompass the devil in the play it did, and after his death even his riches reverted to his Christian son-in-law, Lorenzo, in Belmont.

The Merchant of Venice must therefore remain a legend, where good in the fairy tale triumphs over evil, where the old gives way to the new. But the achievement of perfectibility can never be part of the human condition. It is high time indeed that discerning readers learn to separate legend from truth and cease from applying unrealistic yardsticks by which to evaluate Shylock and Portia.

3
Jews and Right Reason

THE Merchant of Venice is structured on the contrast between Venice and Belmont, on the antithesis between a crass realistic existence and the idealized spiritual life. But early in the seventeenth century such contrasts were blurred. The "new philosophy," which included a revolutionary scientific appreciation of the physical universe, cast all in doubt. In the Middle Ages, Christianity had bequeathed a sacerdotal view of life to mankind. But now that perspective would explode and shatter into many different angles, upsetting man's view of himself in creation. No longer would he be the center of his known world, a planet about which all the heavenly bodies were revolving. Instead, according to new revolutionary theories of astronomy, man was only an infinitesimal being, temporarily grounded on a minuscule planet, itself spinning dislocatedly in space about an impermanent sun. That great chain of being, stretching heavenward since biblical times, was now full of imperfections. Man could no longer aspire to the divine, if by the cold light of science his reason was merely the extension of matter in motion. In such a world, where human intelligence would count for little, Christian thinkers turned to the very bedrock of Jewish thought to confirm the necessity of man as a vital being in the creation of existence. Seventeenth-century divines and other scholars encountered a matrix of ideas common to the thinking both of the Church Fathers and of some learned Jews, such as Philo and Maimonides. What had appeared to Francis Bacon as an intellectual revolution, that nature was as much God's creation as written Scripture was, in reality, basic to Judaism. The Psalmist of old had already written "The heavens declare the glory of God." And Sir Thomas Browne's opinion that the Divine Law was operative in all creation was but another way of asserting the Jewish view that the universal God was also the God of nature.

Similarly, the Church Fathers, led by Origen, had refashioned the Alexandrian and Rabbinic doctrines that the Scriptures might be interpreted on a multiple level of meanings. But if the founders of Christianity had reinterpreted biblical statements either to confirm or to foreshadow events unique to their religion, their process of reading Scripture to include its literal, moral, analogical, or mystical meaning was but an extension of the well-known Jewish fourfold interpretation of the Bible. Whenever Francis Bacon, Thomas Browne, or John Milton, for example, were confronted with natural truths that did not square with the truths of faith encountered in the Scriptures, they too resorted to the Jewish notion that the Bible was written to accommodate itself to "the language of men." And at such times, when their own intellectual capacities proved inadequate, Bacon and Browne argued, in direct descent from Jewish sources, that the more implausible a miracle, the greater the need to accept it on faith. If Milton insisted on viewing the Scriptures as a moral guide for individual action, this too derived from Jewish origins, that God comes to everyone in terms of his own conscience. John Smith, another seventeenth-century thinker, went further, and openly acknowledged his debt to rabbinic thought. Smith was at one with the rabbis in distinguishing between true and false prophecy.

He noted three gradations of godlike illumination that can

affect men. The first was of a superior quality, as when Moses saw God face to face; the second occurred when man's imagination was stirred by figurative language, capable of correct interpretation; and the last took place when distorted images crowded in upon the mind and resulted in false prophecy, or divination. Smith equated the highest form of prophecy with the "Ruach Hakkodesh," the Holy Spirit, which he, like the Jews, felt was the divine inspiration for Proverbs, Psalms, Ecclesiastes, and the Book of Job. In a humorous aside, Smith managed to preserve his Christianity by observing that the Jews regarded the "Ruach Hakkodesh" as the Spiritus Sanctus,

> not because it flows from the Third person of the Trinity (which, [he] doubted) they thought not of in this business, but because [it signified Holiness and goodness in the hearts of good men.]

It might perhaps be pertinent to inquire whether such views did not destroy the very core of Christianity. What, after all, was to be made of the Fall of Man, if Bacon's observation that Adam's sin consisted not in his search for knowledge but in his decision to "give law unto himself" were to prevail? In Jewish terms his precise sin lay exactly in this: that in making the law for himself he would, by knowing good from evil, play the god. Or how would Smith's modified view of the Third Person of the Trinity accord with accepted Christian doctrine? Such imponderables in terms of traditional Christianity would pale before the writings of a Lord Herbert of Cherbury, who constructed a rational theology devoid of credal qualifications. In this scheme Christ was no longer divine, but was a divinely inspired teacher. He fulfilled the Law, seen first by the Jews in an allegory, then exemplified in the Gospels as a written example for the image of the divine to be realized in man.[1]

However, such alterations in basic Christian thought did

Jews and Right Reason

not make their proponents think of themselves as anything but Christians. Even that arch-materialist Hobbes interlaced his *Leviathan* with spiritual references and requests for conformity in public worship, because in an ordered state dutiful subjects have to obey their sovereign even in matters of religion.

Indeed, the larger part of the seventeenth century reflected the most Christian of climates. All sorts of religious literature flowed from the presses. Royal and middle-class audiences regarded their preachers as lecturers, publicists, and even entertainers. The writings of these divines, whether couched in plain, homespun English or in the crabbed style of the learned metaphysicians, still revolved about the central concepts of Christianity. For all that the burgeoning Anglican establishment represented a blend of the new humanism with a latitudinarian philosophy, the benefits from the application of the lessons of Christianity were not to be granted those in an unconverted state. The infidels, Moslem, Papist and Jew were still lost if they persisted in their original state of lack of grace. John Donne, who forsook the secular follies of his youth to embrace an acceptable Anglicanism, may indeed have merely transferred the metaphysical agonies of human love to his religious love of God. But if Donne were forever wrestling with his God, to approach Him through doubts and perplexities,[2] he still knew that such approaches were vouchsafed only to Christians. This Dean of St. Paul's remained content in the belief that faith in Christ is necessary for the salvation of all men.

> They are too good husbands and too thrifty of God's grace, too sparing of the Holy Ghost, that restrain God's general propitious *venite omnes.* Let all come, and *vult omnes salvos,* God would have all men saved; so particularly as to say, that when God says all, he meanes some of all sorts, some men, some women, some Jews, some rich, some poore, but he does not meane, as he seemes to say, simply All. Yes; God does meane, simply All, so that as no man

can say to another, God meanes not thee, no man say to himself, God meanes not me.[3]

In common with other Anglican preachers, Donne viewed his church as the only universal Establishment; he was willing, of course to admit all. This much-vaunted breadth of interest allowed him to assert with equanimity that only fundamental differences of doctrine justified conversion. Yet such latitudinarianism must in no way be confused with modern recognition of differing points of view. That greatest of Anglican pulpiteers, Jeremy Taylor, may readily have appealed to Scripture and to reason for an end to theological bickering among men, but his appeal was still based on the belief that adhering to the Apostles' Creed and seeking the good Christian life were "necessary to salvation."[4] Taylor never arrived at the Miltonic point of view which would have allowed the individual conscience to take precedence over religious organizations and the written Scriptures. What Taylor and his colleagues did share in common with the Puritan cause, and with this Milton himself was in agreement, was that unregenerate man, subjected eternally to the Mosaic Code and Old Testament legalism, would be born again into grace were he voluntarily to accept Christ's teachings.[5]

In the seventeenth century, this call was renewed with particular vigor both by Christian mystics and fundamentalists, who awaited the millenium with a new-found eagerness, a fulfillment to be realized only with the absorption of Judaism into a victorious Christianity. Depending upon the mood of the Christian caller, the heretics were either to be chastised into the need for return, or urged by the bonds of love to see the light and forsake their evil ways. Despite his eagerness to pursue knowledge to its utmost bounds, Sir Thomas Browne still believed that the Jews' acceptance of Christianity was essential to the true faith. Neither his attempts to subjugate his reason to his faith, and lose himself in an "O Altitudo" of spiritual heights, nor his penchant for seeking scientific solutions to such biblical puzzles as the six days of creation, mitigated the vehemence with which he urged the Jews to renounce their stubborn hold on their own religion.

> I am ashamed...at the rabbinical interpretation of the Jews upon the Old Testament as much as their defection from the New; and truly it is beyond wonder how that contemptible and degenerate issue of Jacob, once so devoted to ethnic superstition, and so eagerly seduced to the idolatry of their neighbors, should now in such an obstinate and peremptory belief adhere to their own doctrine, expect impossibilities, and in the face and eye of the church, persist without the least hope of conversion;
> this is a vice in them that were a virtue in us; for obstinacy in a bad cause is but constancy in a good.[6]

Unlike Browne, George Herbert, mystic and visionary, sought to tie the Jews to the dominant faith by persuasion, though even here his metaphysical wit did not forsake him.

> Poor nation, whose sweet sap and juice
> Our scions have purloined, and left you dry,
> Whose streams we got by Apostle's sluice,
> And use in baptism, while ye pine and die:
> Who by not helping once became a debtor
> And now by keeping lose the letter.

Henry Vaughan was more cheerful; the very future itself pointed to the Jews' conversion, a joyful event, only slightly mitigated by reproach

> O then that I
> Might live, and see the Olive bear
> Her proper branches!....
> For as your fast and foul decays
> Forerunning the bright morning star
> Did sadly note his healing rayes
> Would shine elsewhere, since you were blind,

And would be cross, when God was kinde:
So by all signs
Our fulness too is now come in
And the same Sun which here declines
And sets, will few hours hence begin
To rise on you again, and look
Towards old Mamre and Eshcol's brook.[7]

Abraham Cowley, who, like Milton saw a divine imperative in the poet's calling, insisted that only two items were lacking for the fulfillment of the millenium; one, the use of biblical materials as sources for poetic inspiration, and two, the conversion of the Jews.[8]

Such emphasis on the need for justice of conversion should refute any notion that the Puritans, in their zeal for fundamentalist interpretations of the Old Testament, were some sort of new Jew writ large. Were this true, the image of the old Jew could have been left to die of its own irrelevancy. But this was not to be. Though some Puritans might have adhered to Old Testament laws, and other Protestants, by adopting Sabbatarian practices, might have been imprisoned for Judaizing, Puritanism and Judaism were two vastly differing orientations to life. Nothing in Judaism accepted the doctrine of determinism, or conferred salvation upon the elect, two views essential to the core of Puritanism. And if Puritanism tried to fashion the daily life of its adherents around the tenets of the Old Testament, Judaism had centuries ago, through the Mishnah and Talmud, evolved a civilization removed both in time and space from certain ways of life enumerated in the Old Testament.

It is indeed true that Mishnaic and Talmudic influences ought to be taken into account when considering Milton's knowledge. He based his view of divorce on rabbinic sources. Parallels in Kabbalistic and other Jewish writings have been found for certain passages in *Paradise Lost*, particularly where Satan assumes varying bestial forms to tempt Eve, and where she, in turn, decides to persuade Adam to eat the fruit of the tree of knowledge. Yet when all is said and done, Milton's *Of Christian Doctrine*, a prose exposition of his religious beliefs, remains the basis for *Paradise Lost,* so that his view of Adam's transgression was at odds with the Jewish interpretation. In the epic, Adam's sin consists primarily in crossing God's will. But in Judaism the eating of the apple itself is far from an indifferent matter; consuming the fruit is inevitably linked with the evil that the act connotes. Adam had bent the law to his own purpose; therein, in Jewish terms, lay his sin. But in *Paradise Lost* a whole scope of implications of the Fall is what makes it Christian in nature. Nothing in Judaism went on to connect the Fall with a matrix of ideas about which the concepts of original sin and redemptive grace through Christ might cluster. Whether the Fall here is viewed psychologically, as a perverse condition into which man has maneuvered himself, or figuratively, as symbolic of man's loss of holiness, *Paradise Lost* remains the most Christian of epics.[9]

Similarly, it would at first glance be easy to insist that Milton, in those prose passages written in the full flush of his millenarian hopes, rooted his concept of justice in what was a Hebraic milieu.

> O perfect and accomplish thy glorious acts! for men may leave their works unfinished but thou are a God, thy nature is perfection, shouldst thou bring us thus far onward from Egypt to destroy us in this wilderness though we deserve, yet thy great name would suffer in the rejoicing of thine enemies and in the deluded hope of all thy servants. When thou hast settled peace in the Church and religious judgment in the kingdom then shall all thy saints address their voices of joy and triumph to thee, standing on the shore of that Red Sea into which our enemies had almost driven us. And he that now for haste snatches up a plain ungarnished present as a thank-offering to thee which could not be deferred in regard of thy so many late deliverances wrought for us one upon another, may then perhaps take up a harp and sing thee elaborate song to generations. In

that day it shall no more be said as in scorn this or that was never held so till this present age, when men have better learnt that the times and seasons pass along under thy feet to go and come at thy bidding.

Yet Milton himself never forsook that world perspective basic to all Christianity.

and as thou didst dignify our father's days with many revelations above all the foregoing ages since thou tookest the flesh; so canst thou vouchsafe to us (though unworthy) as large a portion of thy Spirit as thou pleasest: for who shall prejudice thy all-governing will? Seeing the power of thy grace is not passed away with primitive times as fond and faithless men imagine, but thy kingdom is now at hand and thou standing at the door. Come forth out of thy royal chambers, O Prince of all the Kings of the earth! put on the visible robes of thy imperial majesty, take up that unlimited sceptre which thy Almighty Father had bequested thee; for now the voice of thy bride calls thee, and all creatures sigh to be renewed.[10]

Ultimately, even such liberties as Milton may have taken with traditional Christian dogma—his concept of God's creating the world out of chaos, his radical views on accepted notions of the Trinity, his virtual silence on the matter of Christian miracles, and his implied rebellion against the Puritan issues of free will and predestination— in no way diminished the the essentially Christian nature of the new world Milton envisioned.

now unite us entirely...tie us everlastingly in willing homage to the prerogative of thy eternal throne...amidst the hymns and hallelujahs of saints, someone may celebrate thy divine mercies...in this land thoughout all ages; whereby this great and warlike nation...inured to the fervent and continual practice of that high and happy emulation to be found the soberest, wisest and most *Christian [i.m.]* people at that day, when thou the eternal and shortly expected King, shalt open the clouds to judge the several kingdoms of the world, and distributing national honors and rewards shall put an end to all earthly tyrannies.[11]

It seems obvious, then, that Christian thinkers, either in voicing their hopes for a millenium, based in part on the conversion of the Jews, or on a return to scriptual origins, had not really intended any purposive reevaluation of the concept of the Jew. Yet the Puritans, who were Calvin's legal heirs in England, did forge ahead to modify some of the medieval aspects of Christian-Jewish relationships. This was due in part to Calvinism's new espousal of modern capitalist economic theories, which erased some of the medieval restrictions on trade with Jews. Such alterations in social and economic contacts between Christians and Jews also grew from Protestantism's call to liberty of conscience, flowing from the power of individual interpretation of Scripture. It would be folly to assume that these tendencies were absolutes whose dictates removed all restrictions from Jews and other non-believers at one fell swoop. In his appeal to freedom of conscience, Milton had urged Cromwell,

> after having endured so many sufferings and encountered so many perils for the sake of liberty not to suffer it, now it is obtained either to be violated (by himself), or in any one instance impaired by others.[12]

In this connection it would be well to remember that the idealistic Roger Williams advocated the natural rights of all men, including Jews and atheists, in his *Bloody Tenent of Persecution*. His monograph was publicly burned because he had embraced such radical ideas. Shortly thereafter he found the English temper so uncompromising that he was forced to flee to the New World. Williams was more courageous in this regard than James Harrington, who in his utopia, *Oceana*, was prepared to settle dispersed Jews in remote Ireland, but was still determined to bar them, Catholics, and pagans, from such equalities as were conferred upon them by his imaginary republic.[13]

In the larger sense neither Milton's guiding principle of conscience nor the Quaker's inner light offered any protection to those whom the Puritan establishment scorned. The progressive elimination of figurative concepts of truth, in favor of a new view of God as right reason, should indeed have fostered the belief in the basic worth of the individual. But in England of the seventeenth century, hundreds of individuals had been burned at the stake as witches and as the devil's sorcerers. The doctrine of religious liberty, which ultimately implied political equality and individual freedom, was proclaimed only by certain fearless Independents and other left-wing Puritans. The right-wingers in the Party, the Presbyterians, held to strict systems of church organization, and, like their Calvinist forebears, frowned on any notions of popular government.[14] While Cromwell stood with the Independents in matters of liberty and conscience, he was not yet prepared to accept

> such a broad toleration of all men as to countenance those who deny the divinity of our Savior or to bolster up any blasphemous opinions contrary to the fundamental verities of religion.[15]

It was therefore all the more astonishing that Cromwell, having little use for Anglicans and less for Catholics, should have allowed the Jews to reside legally in England. But he had always been concerned with strengthening English commerce against the monopolistic practices of the Dutch and the Spaniards. Cromwell knew full well that during the reign of Charles I there already were prosperous Jews, refugees from inquisitorial Spain and Portugal, who were quietly pursuing their mercantile careers in London. Nominally, for their own protection, they were still Catholics, but they revealed Jewish sympathies. At the same time, the Antwerp and Amsterdam Jewish communities had acquired significant positions in world trade. They had international connections. Some of the representatives of Dutch financial corporations were operating in London. Other spokesmen were influential in the West Indian trade. Such factors could have weighed heavily in England's favor in her economic rivalries with Holland and Spain.

Meanwhile, a series of events had undermined the Established Church in England and encouraged the growth of various Protestant sects. A few of these were prepared to extend toleration to the Jews for several reasons. Though they were in the minority, some theologians regarded Britain's national difficulties as just punishment for its past persecutions of the Jews. Many more clergymen, as noted before, believed that conversion was a necessary prelude to the long-awaited millenium.

Such ideas coincided in part with the observations of a well-known Dutch rabbi, Manasseh ben Israel, who petitioned Cromwell and his Council of State to readmit the Jews to England. The rabbi insisted that the presence of Jews in England would be the last remaining requisite to fulfilling the biblical prophecy concerning their dispersion to the ends of the earth. Such a condition, in accordance with tradition, was necessary to insure the Messiah's hoped-for arrival.

Finally, Cromwell responded by neither confirming nor denying the Jews' formal right to return to England. Instead, he opened the entire issue to deliberation at a conference in Whitehall in December 1655. There he listened to the religious expositions of conservative and reactionary divines who suspected that the presence of Jews in the land would undermine Christianity. He also, as we shall see, appeared sensitive to the complaints of London merchants and politicians who feared economic competition from a large Jewish population. Midway through these proceedings, Cromwell abruptly ended the conference. It was not reconvened.

Other events in the Spring of 1656 finally forced the issue of Jewish settlement. By then, England was again at war with

Spain, so that the property of all Spaniards residing in England was to be expropriated. This forced some twenty-odd Marrano families in London to renounce their Spanish origins and reaffirm their Judaism. They did so by asking Cromwell to help them. They wished now to be able to worship privately as Jews and to purchase land for a cemetery. In petitioning Cromwell these Jews had rallied to the support of one of their neighbors, Antonio Rodriguez Robles, who stood to lose his entire fortune were he to persist in regarding himself as a Catholic of Spanish origin. Once Robles and the others explained their predicament, the English government acknowledged them as Jewish refugees. They were allowed to keep their property intact. During the summer of 1656 their requests for the right to worship as they pleased and to bury their dead in accordance with their own customs had been granted to them. The privilege of legal residence in England had thereby been confirmed implicitly rather than explicitly.

It is believed that by June 26, 1656, Cromwell dispatched messengers to the Rabbi, informing him of this result. But in truth the Rabbi's original petition had not actually been answered. By responding instead to the more practical requests of the Marranos-turned-Jews, Cromwell had acted in a spirit of omission rather than commission. He simply had never formalized the readmission of Jews to England. This is further proof that he must have been aware of the strong opposition to Jewish settlement during his incumbency.[16]

With the return of Charles II to the English throne, Jews were again protected, this time by royalty, from the attempted restrictions on their religion by English xenophobes. Charles may not have been moved by Puritan millenarianism, but he was prepared to repay the Jews for loans they had made to him while he was in exile in France.[17]

The famous diarists of the period, John Evelyn and Samuel Pepys, were aware of the arrival and settlement of the Jews in England. Evelyn's entry in his diary for December 1656 was in the very month when Jews began synagogue services in a house in Creechurch Lane, which they had renovated for that purpose. Several years later Pepys reached there, and was duly appalled at the apparent lack of decorum at a religious service. Historians now realize that he must have visited the synagogue one evening in the fall of the year, during a particularly gay Jewish holiday, when the year's scriptual readings in the synagogue had been completed, with the cycle scheduled to start again. Prior to resuming their reading from Genesis, the Jews literally danced in the aisles with the Scrolls of the Law. Astute observer that he was, Pepys saw it all:

> After dinner my wife and I, by Mr. Rawlinson's conduct, to the Jewish synagogue; where the men and boys in their veils and the women behind lattice out of sight; in some things stand up, which I believe is their law in a press, to which all coming in do bow; and in the putting on their veils do say something, to which others that hear them do cry Amen, and the party do kiss his veil. This service all in a singing way, and in Hebrew. And anon their laws that they take out of the press are carried by several men, four or five several burdens in all, and they do relieve one another; and whether it is that everyone desire to have the carrying of it, thus they carried it round about the room while such service is singing. And in the end they had a prayer for the King, which they pronounced his name in Portuguese, but the prayer like the rest in Hebrew. But Lord, to see the disorder, the laughing, the sporting and no attention, but confusion in all their service, more like brutes than people knowing true God, would make a man foreswear over seeing them more; and indeed I never did see so much, or could have imagined there had been any religion in the world so absurdly performed as this.[18]

Pepys had obviously seen the Jewish community in one of its more unrestrained moments. But in general it was comprised of sober business men engaged mostly in wholesale commerce, since retail trade was still forbidden them. It was a community, self-disciplined to a rigid code of Orthodox Jewish piety and learning, one given to excommunicating any of its members who did not adhere to its strict communal standards of public worship and behavior, and high personal standards of business ethics. It had absorbed the thoroughness of its former inquisitorial masters and watched constantly for backsliders. It allowed for about as much freedom of conscience within the confines of its own jurisdiction as did its Puritan hosts, which is to say, a minimal amount.

Judging from another one of Pepys's entries, it would seem that the Jewish community in England was much affected by some of those incidents in which their coreligionists on the Continent were involved. The year of the great Fire of London, 1666, was also the year in which Sabbatai Zevi, one of the Jewish pseudo-Messiahs, fanned flames of religious ardor everywhere, including England. Pepys recorded the following incident in February of that year.

> I am told for certain, what I have heard once or twice already, of a Jew in town, that in the name of the rest offered to give any man 10 pounds to be paid a hundred pounds, if a certain person now in Smyrna be within these two years owned by all the princes of the East, and particularly the grand Signor, as the King of the world, in the same manner we do the King of England here, and that this man is the true Messiah. One named a friend of his that had received 10 pieces of gold upon this score, and says that a Jew has disposed of 1100 pounds in this manner, which is very strange; and certainly this year of 1666 will be a year of great action: but what the consequences of it will be, God knows.[19]

The millenial hopes of the betting Jewish gentleman had dissolved to nothingness, as had those of the Fifth Monarchy men a decade before, in the heyday of Puritanism. The Christian humanism of the Taylors, the Halls, and the Hookers on the one hand, and the Miltons and some of the Cambridge Platonists on the other, likewise failed to lead to a rejuvenated Messianic world where the Jews were to be the final witness to the new revelations. Instead, the cynicism, wit, scorn, refined rationalism, and dissolute morals that characterized the literature of the Restoration came to the fore. When the theaters were reopened after the Puritan hiatus, all the ugly old medieval stereotypes of the Jew reappeared. That emphasis on the Jew as the devil's representative then gave way, particularly in the literature of the Augustan Age, to the caricature of the Jew as the unscrupulous money dealer. This theme was to reveal itself in the new-found art of journalistic fiction, one that perhaps took its initial clue from the financial prosperity in which some leaders of the Jewish community found themselves.

Such affluence assured that community a certain degree of protection through its access to the Crown. Throughout the second half of the seventeenth century, whenever there were attempts, either by merchants or politicians, to hamper the Jews in their trade, restrict them in their worship, or discriminate aginst them politically through the imposition of special taxes, the kings of England would usually intervene in their behalf. Through the simple expedient of royally enforced delay, anti-Jewish legislation would merely die a natural death.

In addition to such advantages as accrued to the Jewish community from the sheer absence of negative ordinances, certain legal enabling acts furthered their rights as residents in the land. In the latter decades of the seventeenth century, Jews were allowed to give evidence in courts of law and take their oaths on the Hebrew Bible. They were released from the necessity of being present in court on their Sabbath and, finally, a judge decided that Judaism as a religion was no longer a sufficient obstacle to prevent a plaintiff from bringing suit in court to recover his debts. After the Jews had been instrumental in financing the accession of William of Orange to the English throne in 1688, an attempt in Parliament to suppress blasphemy was so designed as to exclude Jews from its intent.[20]

All these factors augured well for the future political and economic well-being of the Jews.[21] But social discrimination against them was still based on their seemingly foreign traits, and on ascriptions of insularity to them. For this reason the literary image of the Jew that emerged in the eighteenth century relied on his peculiarities for its effectiveness.

4
Jews and Middle-Class Culture

*I*N Amsterdam, Jews had been the traders, financiers, and factors, helping Holland launch her overseas empire. Once they reached England, the more affluent members of the community followed similar occupations. As wholesalers in the import-export trade, they imported bullion and staples from the Levant in return for English woolens. Others were brokers and stockjobbers. In a short while the small community of Jews in London received additional members from Germany and Easten Europe. They were not all wealthy. Some of the immigrants were unemployed. And there were complaints that non-Jewish aliens were subsidized by the synagogue. But because official representatives of the Jewish community were well-to-do merchants and traders, the belief persisted that most Jews were affluent. Even Sir Roger de Coverley, that genial, fictional creation in Addison and Steele's *Spectator*, admits that with his swarthy complexion he has been mistaken for a Jew in the assembly of stockjobbers at Jonathan's (a coffee house).[1] Shortly before Queen Anne's accession to the throne, twelve members of the Jewish community did have seats on the royal exchange. Later on, the term, *'Change Alley* invariably referred to the place where Jews traded. Some of them achieved national status because of their financial prosperity. One, Benjamin Levy, became a "Proprietor of the Western Division of the Province of New Jersey" and was active in the affairs of the Dutch East India Company. Still another, Solomon Medina, served as a contractor for the British Army. He also paid the Duke of Marlborough an annual fee for intelligence work. Though this contributed to the Duke's political demise, Medina used the information he received from this arrangement to operate a news agency. Medina was knighted for his efforts in the war against France, but he was publically criticized for his association with Marlborough.[2]

No such condemnation was directed against Sampson Gideon, a banker who managed to restore public confidence in government securities when the South Sea land investment scheme collapsed in 1720, and again in 1745, when there was a Jacobite uprising against the ruling monarchy.[3]

The majority of English Jews possessed none of the wealth of a Benjamin Levy, a Solomon Medina, or a Sampson Gideon. Yet the financial ventures of these men and others like them reflected that sense of Renaissance acquisitiveness which Calvin and his Puritan heirs in England had unwittingly helped to project into their own times and beyond. Much earlier, Christopher Marlowe had signaled both the fascination and horror with which the Christian world regarded Barabas. He, by his wiles, helped to control kings and make history, while he yet accumulated riches. Now, the whole Calvinist understanding of the uses of money was, for all its modifications, part of the outgrowth of just such a Renaissance point of view: man had the power through his wisdom and reason to put all the physical and material resources of the universe to work for him. No longer would it be unnatural for gold, a "barren metal" to add to its own worth. In Calvin's world, and later in the Puritan and modern worlds, such gold would indeed breed. Charging interest, newly viewed as a legitimate aspect of economic activities, reflected the expansionist spirit in trade and commerce. This attitude made itself felt in Restoration London, found ample expression in eighteenth-century colonialism, and finally reached its total justification in nineteenth-century British imperialism.

A whole set of circumstances had combined to make the Jews of Western Europe the natural agents in this development of capitalism. Even since the medieval Church had forced them to base their wealth not on land, Jews had to rely on their movable assests—gold bullion, gems, and precious metals—as sources of credit. At the same time, they gained invaluable experience at those occupations normally forbidden to practicing Christians, namely, lending money at interest, speculating, and manipulating the intricacies of foreign exchange. Having earlier been the financial agents to feudal chieftains, Jews now easily slipped into the role of banker. Centuries of perusing Talmudic law, with its emphasis on accepted modes of logical analysis, had equipped Jews with the ability to reason by means of tightly constructed arguments. This propensity for developing sound premises, reached in the give and take of dialectical statements, and far removed from matters of personal or emotional satisfaction, would now serve them in good stead in those speculative maneuvers so necessary to the world of high finance. Unremitting persecution and forced banishments led to their dispersal throughout the Old World, but these events also helped fashion contacts for them with Jews and non-Jews, contacts that were universal in scope. There were other factors that also contributed to their unique adeptness at financial matters. Because of the early historic restrictions forbidding them from working on the land, Jews had had many centuries at their disposal in which to become accustomed to the sophisticated processes of urban existence. They were prepared to employ all their wits about the business of making money for kings and governments. Perhaps this might explain how it was possible for Sampson Gideon, one of the twelve "Jew brokers" on the royal exchange, to have handled "one quarter of all the public loans negotiated by the British government" (during the reigns of King William and Queen Anne).[4]

As financial advisers and counselors to governmental officials, Jews benefited from the economic freedom that now flowed from this basically Renaissance approach to the uses of wealth.[5] Logically, in such a scheme, the Jews should then have been regarded as collaborators in a new world whose vast resources were there, ready for man's discovery and use. But centuries of theological differences, sharpened by dark, emotional discolorations, dictated otherwise. The portrait of the Jew in English literature that now emerged was still darkened, but the focus had shifted. The medieval stereotype of the Jew as devil-usurer had altered to become that of a usurer. Such meager references to Jews as there were in Restoration drama harped on this theme, while the philosophic impulses of the Age of Reason gave it new breadth, and it became a staple for character renditions in the emerging novels of this period.

Whenever the Jew appeared, whether it was on the stage, in satirical essays, in highly structured poetry given to fine ratiocinations, or in the new genre of the novel, he was no longer the old devil of the miracle plays. Medieval charges that Jews spread the plague by poisoning wells and that they killed children were matters of the past. Those earlier calls for conversion as matters of public policy had also diminished. But, consonant with the new fashion of the times, dislike for the Jew took its cue from the prevailing emphasis upon wit and from cool appeals to human reason. In such an atmosphere Jews and their relationship to society had somehow to be reduced and trivialized. This was to be accomplished through the art of caricature. There were to be no Barabases lurking about eighteenth-century drama. For in periods of reason and order, men are not likely to endow their villains with the ability to enact deeds of earth-shaking proportions. Literary portraits of Jews that now appeared were of merely villainous misers, but pale shadows of their forebears once portrayed as vile perpetrators of unimaginable horrors. Accordingly, all the monetary finagling and financial duplicity indulged in by Jewish characters in drama, prose, and fiction diminished to inconsequential proportions. Instead of intriguing about the downfall of kingdoms, Jewish moneylenders in eighteenth-century literature were expected to expend their wealth on maintaining loose women for their personal pleasure, or to use their monies to gain entrée into society. In real life, however, there were social contacts between several enormously wealthy Anglo-Jewish families and some English peers.[6] Such relationships then became the subjects of literary conventions, where inevitably the impoverished nobleman was indebted to the Jew.

On occasion, the Jews' material assets would turn their possessors into fops and dandies who, even as they aged, did not abandon their effete ways. Transforming villains into beaux brummels then inaugurated a tradition that flowered in the next century. More immediately, as the decades of the seventeen hundreds sped by, buffoons and sharpers were added to the literary image of the Jewish money-mad characters. To describe the eccentricity of all these dolts, writers portrayed them as gesticulating ranters in dirty clothes. Their speech was reduced to some foreign jargon or a form of unintelligible gibberish. Their evil had become utterly slight and meaningless. It had lost all its tragic overtones. Like Milton's Lucifer, the medieval Jew-devil had by now shrunk to the size of a toad. George Granville's Shylock in *The Jew of Venice* was just such an odious nonentity who wondered from which part of Antonio's body it were best to cut the pound of flesh. In his lighter moments, this Shylock, banqueting, would propose a toast to his mistress's money. In Dryden's last play, *Love Triumphant*, a stupid, converted Jew, Sancho, himself a usurer's son and out to marry for money, became the butt of the comedy.

Because Jews were supposed to talk arrant nonsense,

Dryden's contemporary, William Congreve, in *The Way of the World* had one of his witless fops, Witwoud, in a scene built on the extreme inanities to which the uses of language may be put, declare that "contradictions beget one another like Jews." And in *The Double Dealer*, a wife deriding her husband finally compares him, in an ever-descending order of contempt, to "Turk, Saracen and Jew."[7]

Wealthy Jews, who received their just deserts for keeping Christian mistresses, provided another favorite theme in the dramatic entertainment of the time. Theophilus Cibber, in his pantomime *The Harlot's Progress*, based on William Hogarth's six engravings called *Harlot's Progress*, used such clowning to great advantage, as did Henry Fielding in his play *Miss Lucy in Town*. There the Jew, who was prepared to buy a Christian wife from her new husband for two hundred guineas, is kicked off the stage for his pains. In still another play, Charles Macklin's *Love à la Mode*, the Jew's role as lover was transformed. He was obligated to play one among three other suitors for a rich woman's hand. This gave the author an opportunity to catalogue the suitors' traits in ethnic and racial terms.[8] In the process the Jew is insulted most frequently; as always, he is treated as an alien.

Richard Brinsley Sheridan, a famous Irish dramatist, also fashioned Isaac Mendoza, a Spanish Jew, as the fool in the comedy *The Duenna*. Mendoza was rich, vulgar and stupid, though he imagined himself to be quite cunning. He was therefore properly deceived into marrying a hideous old woman disguised as his beautiful intended bride.

However, even Sheridan's sense of dramatic satire was blunted by that vogue for sentimentality which emerged in the latter half of the eighteenth century. His Jewish broker in *The School for Scandal* was still eager to teach a Christian how to cut corners in a sharp money deal, but his Moses had grown honest. As part of the play's resolution, Moses would be charged with the financial rehabilitation of its young Christian hero.

Attitudes of toleration toward Jews and other declassed people that arose in Germany now mingled with romantic conceptions in literature. These euphemized the importance of the individual. In England at that time, Richard Cumberland applied this new notion to his characterization of an unbelievably virtuous, lonely, old Jewish miser, Sheva. In his play *The Jew*, Cumberland tried to make amends for all the past mistreatment to which Sheva and his co-religionists had been subjected. To achieve his goal, Cumberland concentrated upon Sheva's paradoxical behavior. The old miser starved himself to sustain a newly married Christian couple. The motives for his strange actions were shaped by the need to fulfill a personal obligation and by the demands of true goodness. Sheva was thankful to the brother of the bride, whose father had long ago saved him from an auto-da-fé in Cadiz, Spain. In idealistic terms the play also served Cumberland's purpose when he expatiated on the virtues of the Jews as a perpetually mistreated race. But it is all heavy-handed and humorless, and its characters, including Sheva, appear to be inanimate! Perhaps for these reasons, the local Jewry in late eighteenth-century England did not appreciate Cumberland's efforts on its behalf. He was deeply pained by its indifference to his drama.[9]

The original for Cumberland's Sheva is unknown, though the author credited one of his earlier portrayals, Mr. Abrahams, a kind Jewish merchant, with that honor. A good Jewish moneylender, an improbable character himself, in one of Tobias Smollett's novels, *The Adventures of Ferdinand, Count Fathom*, may also have inspired Cumberland to fashion a benevolent usurer.[10]

No such problems of origin attached themselves to the objects of Jonathan Swift's scorn. Much earlier in the century, long before Sheridan and Cumberland had even imagined that good Jews existed, Swift was damning them all— good, bad, or indifferent. In fact, Swift disparaged all peoples who were different from him. The low opinion he held about Jews merely confirmed his general misanthropy. For him Jews were as evil as Dissenters, who, in turn, were "mavericks," straying from the true faith, Anglicanism. In one of his more zealous moments, Swift thought of these erring individuals as "Aeolists," religionists replete with a windy theology. These were, in fact, characters sprung full-blown from Swift's own madcap imagination. But if his creatures were fantastic, the venom with which they were conceived was real. He made his hatred of all nonconformists explicit when he worried over the consequences were the Jews to join the Catholics and others in a plot to destroy the Church of England.

> What if the Jews should multiply and become a formidable party among us? Would the dissenters join in allegiance with them likewise, because they agree already in some general principles, and because the Jews are allowed to be a stiff-necked and rebellious people?[11]

Swift was firmly convinced that the Jews' deceitfulness in financial matters assured them monetary success at all times, even when stock market prices were falling. Alexander Pope thought even less of Jews. He assumed that obsession with money was their one concern.

Always complaining, Pope frequently attacked his literary colleagues and others associated with the book trade. Once he turned his vicious pen on a particularly disreputable bookseller, Edmund Curll, and rendered an obscene account of how that dealer, greedy for gold, converted to Judaism. In the process, he was subjected to severe physical mutilation, which Pope equated with circumcision. Pope used this tale to warn other Christians against the temptations to which avarice leads.[12]

For its effectiveness, the moral of Pope's ridiculous report depended, as does all satire, on the brilliance with which the discrepancy between the ideal and the actual way of life was to be handled. In that sense, both Pope and Swift were among the great satirists of the English Age of Reason. In the end Swift so despaired of that chasm between the real and the ideal that his satire descended to savagery. For him, the opportunities that a divinely ordered and reasonable Nature could have bestowed on man were expended on the *Houyhnyhymns*, a race of noble horses, while humanity became brutalized to the level of beasts, or *Yahoos*. Certainly, in such a topsy-turvy world, no image of the Jew that could possible have been projected would have had any effect on Swift.[13]

But unlike Swift, Pope professed himself bound to the dictates of the Age of Reason. In fact, in his *Essay on Man* he painstakingly versified an eighteenth-century version of the great chain of being, where Reason reigns supreme and the Divine Machine functions smoothly with no interruption, and where "whatever is, is right." In such a world even the alien Jews have their proper place. Pope argued that God governs by "general not particular laws," so that inequalities among men are inevitable. Such differences are to be minimized by striving for an internal happiness, a virtue that is its own reward. Pope found a spot for the "poisonous herb." He sweetened its effect when he insisted that even evil may be necessary to complement the mystery of God's ultimate beneficence.[14] By accounting for the Jews in a negative fashion, Pope modified the medieval view that consigned them to the devil. His approach was a variation upon the Elizabethan belief; there, the Jew fitted into the dreary, sublunary universe, to be forever excluded from the shining, illusionary realm of Belmont.

No such philosophical underpinning was necessary to justify the image of the Jew, that, with few exceptions, prevailed in the new art form of the period, the novel. Here, even that unique thrust of the Augustan Age, so neatly summed up in all those descriptions of sweet reason and clarity, proved irrelevant. It is true that the eighteenth century was able to reaffirm the place of Nature in God's scheme of creation. And it is likewise valid that all the great thinkers from

Bacon and Descartes to Boyle and Newton confirmed the semingly miraculous, yet reasoned, operations of Divine Law in Nature, so that the mysteries of traditional Christianity fell by the wayside. Yet, if a rationalized Belmont was at last crystallized in the common light of day, that light shed no glow, but rather glared, at the image of the Jew. Those who now focused on the Jew were that new breed of novelist who cared little for the brittle eloquence and surface wit of courtly circles. For them, as for their aristocratic colleagues in the literary arts, the Jew was still an outcast, to be sneered at and reviled.

Life among the landed gentry, the rising merchant class, the small shopkeepers, and the rogues of society became the text for the hack writers in Grub Street. What they all shared in common was that the Jew was still the peddler, the crooked dealer, the financial manipulator, and the alien, to be noted for his peculiarities of speech, dress, and manner.

In his prose and fiction, Daniel Defoe, an early eighteenth-century hack writer, journalist, tradesman, and political spy, credited all Jews with these unsavory roles. His differences with them seem to have been both personal and economic. He may have been in debt to Jewish moneylenders.[15] Moreover, as a true follower of Calvin, he shared his regard for the uses to which wealth might be put, provided that the rates of interest were moderate. Defoe's bookkeeping mind reinforced his uncanny gift for verisimilitude by having Robinson Crusoe and Roxana forever reckon up their material assets. Roxana, because of her membership in the world's oldest profession, measured her wealth in thousands of pounds, yet she was still an outcast in society, to be classed with rogues everywhere. In that sense, her riches were not to be equated with the assets of the monied class, though she herself aspired to the status of an aristocrat. That was sufficient for Defoe to distinguish between ill-gotten gains on the part of the poverty stricken, and the wealth amassed by others, who conceived of investment banking on an international scale. But Jews, like Huguenots and some Quakers, had long been allied with merchant adventurers, lineal descendants of Renaissance entrepreneurs who thought of gold as an international commodity. We recall that Jewish financiers helped negotiate a large portion of a loan for the Bank of England. Defoe distrusted all such evidence of corporate wealth; once he even proposed a scheme to withdraw deposits and eliminate bank credit. He wanted to abolish monopoly capitalism, long favored by the Anglican Church and the Royal Establishment. Yet his Puritan animus against those who practiced investment banking did not extend to the Quakers. Though they were relatively late arrivals on the monetary scene, they too, like the Jews, came to be involved in a type of capitalism noted for economic ventures in matters of "open war, government contracts, state monopolies, speculative promotions and...[financing royal] projects."[16] Yet Defoe's heroes and heroines, especially Moll Flanders, Captain Singleton, and Roxana, were given comfort by Quakers and helped by them to forsake their criminal ways. One can only deduce that Defoe's hatred for Jews was a deeply personal matter.

This showed up again in his novel *Roxana; Or, The Fortunate Mistress*. There he equated an unnamed Jew who was involved with the whore Roxana in a jewel transaction, with the devil. Defoe made the Jew's fiendish physical appearance seem all the more realistic by detailing his gross bodily contortions.

As would befit a devil, the Jew first attempted to rob Roxana of those jewels left in her possession after the murder of her first lover, a jeweler. But the Jew's plans were thwarted by an honest Dutch merchant, whom he later harassed. His subsequent scheme to convict Roxana and prosecute the Dutchman as an accessory to the jeweler's murder then ended in failure. After his ears had been cut off by a French nobleman, the Jew was imprisoned. His last escapade to rob a rich Parisian banker also came to nothing. But this time the

Jew fled and was not heard from again.[17] Defoe's Jews were all vile and greedy. Their distinctiveness lay only in the designation that they were Jews. As such, they were expected to play the role of the villain, alternating between evil and avarice on the one hand, and clowning and lunacy on the other.

On an earlier occasion, Defoe's anti-Semitism was revealed in a theological context. Robinson Crusoe, overtaken by evangelical fervor, attempted to convert his man Friday to Christianity. But Crusoe was hard put to explain the devil to Friday and ended the lesson by trying to turn instead to an emphasis on Christianity's power of salvation. He explained to Friday

> Why our blessed redeemer took not on him the nature of angels, but the seed of Abraham...that he came only to the lost sheep....

Jews never thought of themselves as being tainted by original sin, and therefore the whole issue of salvation did not apply. But in the Christian sense, Jews were regarded as lost. Thus Defoe's affirmation of basic Christianity to Friday detailed the gap between the Jewish and Christian approaches to life.[18]

Defoe's younger contemporary Tobias Smollett was gifted with a savage imagination, was obsessed with the scatological, and possessed an unparalleled capacity to relish the absurd. For him, any characterization at variance with the common run of men became a veritable treasure of clay to be molded to his own artistic purpose. In his best-known work, *The Expedition of Humphrey Clinker*, the lovelorn swain, Wilson, wished to pursue the heroine on her journey to Bath. He arrived at the inn disguised as a Jewish peddler, selling spectacles. The passing reference in the scene to the Jew was calculated to emphasize the oddity of his get-up and behavior, so that the lover, masked as the "rascally Jew," frightened a poor servant girl into hysterics when she saw him.[19] This plan served the author's purpose well. He was thereby able to withhold the lover's true identity until the novel had run three quarters of its course. Because the reader in this instance knew that the disguise was purposely intended, Smollett had no need to expatiate on the legendary evil of the Jew. That he reserved for another work, *The Adventures of Roderick Random*. Here Roderick, prior to his impressment into the British Navy, enjoyed the lustiness of English tavern life. Among the rogues and cutthroats he encountered, there was also Isaac Rapine, the Jewish money lender, whose equally disreputable woman companion, Jenny Ramper, said to him,

> Speak, you old cent-per-cent fornicator; What desperate debt are you thinking of? Well, Isaac, positively you shall never have my favor till you turn over a new leaf, grow honest and live like a gentleman. In the meantime, give me a kiss, you old fumbler. To which he responded, "Ah! you wanton baggage...you are a waggish girl..."[20]

Insofar as Jews were concerned, Smollett's third novel, *Peregrine Pickle*, merely repeats the ludicrous aspects of *Roderick Random*. In *Peregrine Pickle* there was another anonymous Jew, a Rotterdam merchant whom Peregrine met on his travels in France. This Jew, like his counterpart in *Roderick Random*, was involved in an illicit affair with a French lady of pleasure. Their romantic antics, which revolved about a donkey wandering at will through the corridors and bedrooms of a tavern at night, made for hilarious slapstick. Together with another rogue, the Jew received nothing but pain for his attempts at lovemaking. As a witless fool, the Jew in *Peregrine Pickle* was really indistinguishable from Smollett's other comics. He was set apart from the others merely because he was a Jew, who on occasion displayed an evil, "Israelitish grin."[21]

Two factors, however, seem to have tempered Smollett's

judgments about Jews. One was his mad fancy, the other his sense of comedy. As a master caricaturist, Smollett was given to wild exaggeration and misplaced emphasis to achieve the absurd. He applied this technique not only to Jews, nameless and otherwise, who crept about the peripheries of his picaresque tales, but also to an eccentric Scotsman, Captain Obadiah Lismahago, in *Humphrey Clinker.* Lismahago bore all those repulsive qualities which Smollett, with equal aplomb, ascribed to his fictional Jews—the Christian disguised as a Jewish spectacle salesman, Isaac Rapine, and the duped Jew in *Peregrine Pickle.*

However, when Smollett did include a "benevolent Israelite" in *The Adventures of Ferdinand, Count Fathom*, he trimmed his comic genius to the political winds of the day. Artistically, Joshua Manasseh, the kindly miser in *Count Fathom*, was an insufferable bore. He appeared even duller than his evil counterparts in the monetary professions of eighteenth-century fiction. But because he lent money to deserving Christians, and rescued them from embarrassing financial situations, he was so different from his literary colleagues that he deserves special mention. His unusual activities were owing to the author's recognition that in mid-eighteenth-century England there were some temporary flurries of sympathy for the Jews, inspired by particular political and economic events.[22]

In 1753 the Whig government requested naturalization for British Jews. Smollett himself had been in the employ of Whigs, and so might have drawn this character to suit the moment. The bill passed; its supporters had cited Jewish loyalties to the reigning Hanoverian House at the time of the Jacobite rebellion and also took note of the financial assistance Jewish bankers had extended to the Bank of England to prevent a financial panic. But the populace was opposed to the Naturalization Bill, and the following year it was repealed. Smollett returned to his original point that Jews were cheats and sharpers.[23]

Similarities in plot have been found between *Ferdinand Count Fathom* and a German epistolary novel by Christian Furchtegott Gellert, *The History of the Swedish Countess of Guildenstern*. The German work does contain several honest Jewish brokers, each of whom makes life more bearable for a count taken prisoner by the Russians. And in *Ferdinand Count Fathom* Joshua Manasseh lends money graciously to Melvil, Ferdinand's friend, and helps Melvil when he marries. Several other Christians in the novel also benefit from Joshua Manasseh's good deeds. The Gellert work may well have been the reflection of more tolerant attitudes towards Jews expressed in Germany at that time.[24] But it obviously produced no permanent change in Smollett's appraisal of them.

Samuel Richardson, that prudent little middle-aged thinker who titillated his audiences with stories of sexual intrigue behind a façade of moral imperatives, was one with Smollett, Defoe, Swift, and others, in his estimate of the Jews. In his novel *Sir Charles Grandison*, he portrayed a dissolute Portuguese Jew, Solomon Merceda, who was usually involved in assaulting ladies' honor. Though he hoped, after one sorry incident, to improve his character, this turned out to be a delusion, and he ultimately died as a result of his immorality.

Richardson's earlier, epistolary novel, *Clarissa*, had no Jews in it, and Merceda, the Jew of *Grandison*, was really peripheral to the story. He shared his predilection for lustful attacks upon women of virtue with two other Christian rakes, Bagenhall and Sir Hargrave Pollexfen. That his wound was fatal, while his "companions in iniquity" took longer to die, would again be part of that traditional view of justice due the Jew. But Richardson was not so shrill in his accusations against Jews as were his earlier colleagues, Defoe and Smollett.

Precisely because of his relative indifference to his Jewish characterizations, Richardson helped unwittingly to alter the stereotypic image of the Jew in literature. Both in *Clarissa* and in *Grandison*, he recognized the complexity of human emotions. He did so by revealing the effects of human interaction as often at cross purposes with one another. In his earlier work he achieved a sense of individualization by detailing Clarissa's psychological regression as she prepared for death, her only way to atone for the loss of her virginity at the hands of a heartless lover, appropriatedly called Lovelace. *Sir Charles Grandison*, plotless though it is, manages to focus on whole sets of human reactions among different groups of people— reactions to overriding issues of family relationships, to problems that marriage and children present, and to the roles that upstanding citizens must play in society.

What is suggested here is that Richardson's penchant for introspection and his concern for cause and effect in interpersonal relations were the harbingers of new patterns of writing. These, applied to the image of the Jew, changed the older, archetypal configurations into which Jewish characters had been fitted. The alteration, however, was not one by which all old notions and prejudices concerning the Jews would fall by the way. That never happened except perhaps for one isolated moment, when James Joyce created Leopold Bloom in *Ulysses*. But more immediately, because Richardson was concerned with both the inner and the public person, his characterizations expanded and acquired greater dimensions. Paradoxically enough, his influence may also be traced to a writer whose center of interest was always with external characters, with the relationships between man and society, and with historical processes. Sir Walter Scott, a passionate Scottish nationalist and historian, was concerned basically with the surface aspects of life in his novels.

Scott himself acknowledged his literary debt to Richardson. There are parallels between Scott's Rebecca of *Ivanhoe* and Clarissa: Rebecca's inner turmoil, her constant speculation on her fate, her concern for her own moral integrity evoke memories of Clarissa's progressive expiation for her innocent participation in an assault upon her virtue. Furthermore,

Richardson's theme of a foul lover's abducting a virtuous woman against her will, which is the focal event in *Clarissa* and central to the long-winded, episodic development of *Sir Charles Grandison*, may have been the source for Rebecca's being spirited away by the evil Knight Templar in *Ivanhoe*, Sir Brian de Bois-Guilbert.[25]

Other sources for Rebecca have also been suggested. Popular history has it that Scott, at the suggestion of an American friend, Washington Irving, used Rebecca Gratz, a well-known Jewish woman in Philadelphia, as the model for Rebecca.[26] Perhaps the fact that he may have had a real woman in mind enabled him to humanize his fictional Rebecca, stilted though she was. A strong argument might also be constructed to prove that Jews' daughters in English literature are always more credible as fictional creations than are the stock figures their miserly fathers present. There may well be a greater aura of authenticity to Jessica and Rebecca than to Shylock and Rebecca's father, Isaac of York; Jewish heroines had never had to bear the traditional ascriptions of usurer-devil and Christ-killer as part of their characterizations. They had a wider freedom of choice in their actions. But even such an analysis does not detract from Scott's ability to fashion his Rebecca whole, to realize the springs and sources of her actions.

Throughout the novel, Rebecca, both sensual in her beauty and morally virtuous, acted only from a sense of duty. She was prepared always to defend her integrity of character and be faithful to her heritage. She bespoke a perfection completely out of keeping with her relationship to her penny-pinching father and to the Christian society about her. Scott utilized these two contrasts at all times to show us Rebecca's inner person. It was she who rebuked the Saxon knight, Wilfred of Ivanhoe, who would later serve as her protecter against death, for his chivalric obsession with killing and murder. It was she who revealed the hopelessness of the outworn ideals of knight errantry. She thereby became the herald of the modern age, the harbinger of a period in which the trappings of feudalism would at last reveal the meaninglessness of their forms. Her statements, then, provided measuring rods by which all the failures of medieval Christianity and its system of courtly love may be judged.

Yet Rebecca herself was not a modern fictive creation. She did not talk; she invoked and orated. Her perfection of character and beauty made her a paragon of virtue too good to be true. Yet she did think, and we are privy to her innermost reflections. From a modern perspective, she would appear rigid and implacable, but hers was an integrated personality.

It is all the more remarkable that Scott was able to pull off such a characterization in an implausible novel full of stilted talk, contrived occurrences, concealed identities, surprise endings and irritating interruptions by the author at wrong junctures in the story. Briefly, *Ivanhoe* was the tale of two contrasting civilizations in feudal England. It took place in 1194, when Richard the Lion-Hearted returned in disguise to his homeland. Within this context of competing Norman and Anglo-Saxon claims to England's future, Wilfred of Ivanhoe, son to Cedric, the only remaining Anglo-Saxon leader of consequence, was pitted against three arch-foes: representatives of the knightly orders, of the Norman barons, and of the powerful Norman clergy. The story is told with all the gusto of a medieval romance, and it owes much of its structure to the sprawling eighteenth-century novel. Its plot turns on Ivanhoe's successful defense of the Jew's daughter, Rebecca, to stay her execution as a witch by order of the Grand Master of the Knights Templar, for her part in enticing one of its members, Brian de Bois Guilbert. But in reality, Rebecca, like Clarissa, had successfully foiled de Bois Guilbert's blandishments. She would have preferred death to deflowering at the knight's hands. The story was resolved when Richard the Lion-Hearted came to Ivanhoe's aid in that gallant knight's defense of Rebecca. With King John's conspiracy to wrest power from Richard crushed, and the Norman defeated, Ivanhoe then renewed his troth to his Anglo-Saxon bride, Rowena. The Saxons, through their heir apparent, Athelstane, relinquished their claims to the English throne and pledged assistance to Richard. Isaac and Rebecca, privy to the intrigues to destroy the Norman hold over the country and reassert Richard's sovereignty, then left for Spain, where a kindlier welcome awaited them.

The plot itself, as we have seen, is hopelessly romanticized. Scott dangled titillating notions of what would have to be an illicit love between Rebecca and Wilfred of Ivanhoe for the pleasure of the reader. He himself admitted that such a relationship would have been implausible in a feudal setting. More outrageous was the belief that a Saxon knight might come to the defense of a Jewish woman accused of witchcraft. One has only to think of the fate of Christian witches in those days to realize the improbability of Rebecca's situation, an improbability made even more incredible when her foul abductor, de Bois Guilbert, would offer himself as her champion in the lists, were it not for his careerist ambitions in his knightly Order. Yet Scott's correct evaluation of Jewish-Christian relationships in feudal England and his concern for historical accuracy lent an air of realism to an otherwise unbelievable story.

It is this absorption with matters of social custom that enabled Scott to depict Isaac of York accurately, as the Jewish miser perceived in certain specific ways by feudal society. Therefore, throughout the novel, Isaac was the stereotype of the rapacious money-lender, haggling over the price demanded for his daughter's liberation, while yet protesting that she should die rather than be dishonored. Like Shylock, he, too, was forever counting his monies and protesting his poverty. In the repulsiveness of his physical appearance, he was also at one with his predecessors in Defoe's and Smollett's stories. But Scott's enormous capacity for understanding historic cause and effect enabled him to accept, if not to sympathize with his miser. Personally, Scott had no use for Isaac. Frequently, he censured him for the narrowness of his views and his money-mad obsessions. But Scott understood the reasons that led the Jew to depend on money as a means of livelihood. To that degree he provided a rationale for Isaac's behavior, an explanation that was scarcely ever present in the stories of all the old misers who preceded Isaac, and at best only hinted at in *The Merchant of Venice*.

According to Scott, Isaac's odious behavior was merely the result of Christian attitudes toward him. Issac's vileness served Scott as a mirror in which to reflect the hypocrisy of the various ecclesiastical orders and the fraudulence involved in attempts at converting Jews to the dominant faith.

Yet, nowhere in the story did Scott resolve the problem of how so despicable a father could command the loyalty of so lovely a daughter. Rebecca's faithfulness to old Isaac would long ago have put a Jessica to shame. For Jessica, a shrewd, vain, and heartless flirt stole her father's money and forsook her religious and cultural heritage. But Rebecca, made of sterner stuff, followed Isaac into exile.

Their departure indicated Scott's conviction that there was no room for the Jew even in a reconstructed society growing out of the Anglo-Saxon and Norman civilizations. On an allegorical plane, this search for a new residence also had overtones of the Wandering Jew legend. Rebecca herself was a complex, mysterious character, who, like the Wandering Jew, spoke many languages, knew medicine, and possessed divinely prophetic and didactic gifts.

The legend of the Wandering Jew, who was doomed never to die because of his rejection of Christ at the crucifixion, became very popular in the Middle Ages. There are echoes of it in Chaucer's *Pardoner's Tale*, for example. There the old man who tells the robbers where they may find Death, but who himself can never die, may well be a transformed image of the Wandering Jew.

The legend of the Wandering Jew underwent many changes in its journey from land to land. Whenever the Jew reformed and accepted Christ, his burden was lightened, but he was still doomed to wander over the face of the earth. During his many encounters with different individuals, he acquired a formidable store of knowledge. It was this power that sometimes changed him into a Faustian devil who entered into all sorts of outlandish pacts with his human companions. Several long-forgotten Gothic novels of the nineteenth century elaborated upon this theme.[27] But for a few exceptions, these Wandering Jews did not dwell on the pursuit of wealth for its own sake and were not regarded as merchant princes. The change was to be expected, for their Jewishness and the religious differences that had led to their alienation in the first place were now muted to accomodate their new interest: an avid fascination with all the horrible machinations inherent in the power of a devil. Therefore, any resemblance that Wandering Jews bore to other Jewish archetypes in literature would have been to their characterization as supernatural figures. There were vast differences between the wanderer and the moneybound Jew, capitalist, or thief.

Though the Romantic poets may not openly have affirmed such a distinction, they certainly were aware of it. Coleridge still associated the Jews he had met in London with peddlers dealing in secondhand clothes. These bore no relationship to his old sailor, that ancient mariner whose sin consisted of killing an albatross, a bird of good omen. Like a contrite Wandering Jew, the mariner also saw the light. Confronting his own guilty experience, he finally was able to distinguish between the law of justice and that of love. In common with other Romantics such as Shelley and Southey, Byron saw his Wandering Jew as the rebel defying God and society. For all that he was a murderer and an outcast, Byron's Cain commanded his author's admiration. But Byron had no sympathy for those international Jewish bankers, who presumably manipulated their wealth in such a way as to deny the fruits of revolution to independence-starved Spaniards. In his satire *Age of Bronze*, Byron lashed out against the Holy Alliance, Metternich, and international financiers for allowing France, after the Congress of Verona, to invade Spain to crush a local revolution there.[28]

The association of Jews with money continued unabated in literature throughout the Victorian era. Then the moral earnestness, high seriousness, and evangelical fervor of that period combined to ring new changes on the image of the Jews as moneychangers. But that is a topic more properly reserved for Fagin and Philistinism.

5
Fagin and Philistinism

ROMANTICISM faded before the vast changes in existence that characterized the Victorian period. England's economy, based on coal, steel, and railroads, transformed a largely rural society into an urban one. That alteration was not without its penalties. The blight of industrialism eroded the beauties of the countryside and defaced the cities. There urban areas were divided into separate zones. On one side of town, in slum dwellings devoid of the barest conveniences, factory workers eked out an existence marked by poverty, ill health, and lack of education, and circumscribed by early death. At the other end, the wealthy, fattened by the financial returns of their diversified enterprises, dwelled in isolated glory, blessed by good health, good education, long life, and good friends.

Happiness for the privileged few was measured by material prosperity, by the achievements in foreign policy. But behind the façade of a society prepared to bestow the benefits of its advanced civilization on all who would submit to its yoke, there were violent disagreements. Victorian England was torn apart by conflicts between religion and science and between affirmation and skepticism. There were opposing sets of values for those who relied on the efficacy of the machine as a true mark of progress, and for those who insisted that truly integrated individuals were the only guarantors of a meaningful life in an enlightened country.

Like Samuel Taylor Coleridge and Thomas Carlyle before him, Charles Dickens saw society as an organic whole, and men as intelligent beings gifted with intuition. He scorned the views of those philosophers who thought of individuals as passive receptacles of varied impressions and associations. He also denigrated the disciples of Jeremy Bentham and John Stuart Mill, who, like their mentors, put their trust in applied technology and in the democratic process. Dickens believed that such utilitarian concerns with "progress" were tantamount to anarchy.[1] In practice he subscribed to the ideal that a people had a right to fashion its own destiny, and he willingly lent his name to efforts at reform on judicial issues and in matters of social welfare. But in principle Dickens insisted that men's continued dependence upon technological achievements was a disaster. For him the machine itself was more than a mere symbol of the industrial revolution. It had become one of the means by which privileged people, obsessed with its benefits, acquired unlimited riches.

To reach their goals, fiscal ogres in Dickens's novels oppressed the poor though sheer chicanery and duplicity. What is more, they frequently justified their actions by resorting to a fact-filled, emotionless, utilitarian philosophy. Such villains were not only evil people, but they also put wealth and its uses to evil purposes. And it all began with Fagin, the Jewish thief in *Oliver Twist*. From the seeds of his obsession with stolen jewels and his planned misappropriation of an inheritance, there grew whole hothouses of noxious weeds. These were tended by Dickens's later scoundrels. All of them, both the early grotesques and the more humanly endowed misers and merchant princes of his later novels, became tainted and finally were poisoned by such growths. Their punishment, then, was just, for, like Fagin, they calculated their potential for success not by love, but by financial and utilitarian codes. In his personal life, however, Dickens enjoyed the fruits of materialism and was never averse to lavish and ostentatious display. But he saw no connection between his own fascination with money and the fact that money for the characters of his novels became their passion, so that everything from religion to education to the whole business of living yielded to it.

Oliver Twist, one of Dickens's earlier novels, is the tale of an illegitimate child's search for his lost inheritance and the discovery of his true identity. Innocent and angelic, Oliver encountered evil in the person of Fagin and his murderous associates. There were overtones in Fagin, replete with red beard and hair, of the Jew of the old Morality play. Like his stereotypical predecessor, Fagin functioned both as devil and as miser. As Satan, he tempted the boy. Fagin, true devil that he was, believed that he could inveigle the boy into remaining with him forever. Instead, Oliver, like the innocent child heroes of Dickens's other novels, was saved, not by his own exertions,[2] but by the effects of heavenly grace, manifested through an improbable agent, the prostitute Nancy, herself a member of Fagin's gang.[3]

Unlike Oliver, there was no savior to rescue Little Nell of *The Old Curiosity Shop* in her journey from life to death. But the villain of the piece, the dwarfish moneylender Daniel Quilp, who held Little Nell's grandfather in perpetual debt, bore many resemblances to Fagin. Both were monsters who enjoyed their evil actions to a degree that bordered on the insane. Quilp tried to destroy a ship's figurehead, which, he imagined, resembled his enemy,[4] while Fagin "would suffer his features to resolve themselves into a ghastly grin," so as to frighten Oliver. So fiendish was Fagin that even Bill Sikes, himself a murderer, asked his ferocious dog who barked at the old Jew, whether he didn't know the devil when he was wearing a "great-coat".[5] Yet Fagin was not quite so reprehensible as Quilp. By the time Fagin reached the gallows, he was still human enough "to have grown terrible in all the torture of his evil conscience."[6] In contrast, Quilp, who remained grotesque, malign, and dwarfed throughout, died by sheer accident. Fleeing his pursuers, he went out into the fogbound night, fell into the river, and drowned.

Both villains combined a predilection for evil action with bestiality. Quilp resembled a panting dog, while Fagin's physical characteristics suggested those of a wolf.[7] Such dreadful associations could only intensify a sense of disgust at Quilp's and Fagin's continued absorption with money. As rent collector and moneylender, Quilp held nefarious dealings "on 'Change with men in glazed pads and round jackets pretty well every day,"[8] while Fagin, as thief extraordinary, would gloat over his jewels. Could Dickens's references to men on " 'Change Alley," or to the rapacious pickpocket calculating his assets, have also had the same negative associations as those with which simple, hard-working Christian folk had earlier characterized the money-brokers, many of whom were Jews?

By the time Dickens shaped his other villains and let go of his stereotyped evildoers, his concept of a miser included more than an eccentric hoarder. In *Martin Chuzzlewit* the pair of money-grubbing villains who fatally outsmarted each other still illustrates the theme that love of money is the root of all evil. But in the process they turned into obvious hypocrites, associated with corruption and death. Still relying on caricature, on pathos, and on the peculiarities of human behavior, Dickens's later novels move to deeper, darker values. Here, for example, the child in search of love was rejected by adults who themselves needed love. This was why Paul Dombey, Sr. of *Dombey and Son*, in his concern for class and wealth, brought on the destruction of life itself. His child died for lack of love and understanding, while Dombey, Sr., the merchant price, tried to sustain human relationships on the basis of material considerations.[9] Any notions of love had obviously been alien to Fagin. But what were moments of playfulness for him and Oliver, even interrupting Fagin's repellent attraction to money, had in Dombey disappeared. In their stead, impatience ruled. Dombey was unable to wait until his flowering financial enterprises would span the generations. But his son's death destroyed all such dreams. Because Dombey headed an establishment that would not endure beyond his own lifetime, his self-awareness, the essential element of his inner core of being, had been shattered. Dombey's loss of identity paralleled his child's physical demise.

The actual disintegration of Dombey's complex financial schemes before his death reveals Dickens's sharpened view that it was wrong for money-gatherers to hoard their gains for the future. There was a striking similarity here to Fagin's telling Oliver that those jewels in the strongbox were a safeguard against old age. For Fagin, neither the safeguard nor the old age materialized, while to Dombey's detriment, all that remained was old age, sweetened in the last analysis by an unbelievable paragon of a daughter. When Dombey's countinghouse lay in ruins and his glorious mansion was up for sale, with the servants concerned about their wages, Dickens contrived that the ubiquitous Jew, or a figure closely resembling a Jew, should reappear.

> After a few days, strange people begin to call at the house, and to make appointments with one another in the dining room as if they live there. Especially there is a gentleman, of a Mosaic Arabian cast of countenance, with a very massive watch guard, who whistles in the drawing room, and while he is waiting for the other gentleman, who always has pen and ink in his pocket, asks Mr. Towlinson (by the easy name of 'Old Cook') if he happens to know what the figure of them crimson and gold hangings might have been when new bought.[10]

Plainly, Dickens was unable to disassociate the Jews from monetary activities, particularly when that function involved matters of profit and loss.

More than any other of his novels, *Hard Times* validates

one of Dickens's overriding themes: the last word in depredation was the unholy alliance between money-bound capitalism and the utilitarian philosophy designed to promote logic and stifle emotion in life. In *Hard Times*, the joining of these two forces, the economic and the political, symbolized by the loveless marriage of Thomas Gradgrind's daughter Louisa to the aging entrepreneur Josiah Bounderby, proved dead and sterile. As the fraudulent, self-made man, Bounderby had to insure his status by cementing an allegiance with the Gradgrinds, the head of whose household was a utilitarian pedagogue and parliamentary representative, and therefore a spokesman for the current intellectual thought. But Bounderby's marriage to Louisa Gradgrind did not work out. It was shattered by Louisa's would-be seducer, James Harthouse, whom Dickens fashioned to resemble that old tempter, the devil, with a bit of the Jew about him. Later we shall see how Harthouse's foppish airs were further indications of his depravity. But for the moment, as a luckless aristocrat and political careerist, Harthouse was introduced into the novel to prey upon Louisa's affections and to serve as the devil who would entice Louisa's brother, Tom, into delinquency. Yet, Harthouse was a relatively mild fiend. When his plans were thwarted, he took the advice of a simple and good-hearted girl, Sissy Jupe, and left for a foreign country. To see a dissolute man of the world bow to the request of an innocent girl is unrealistic. But one of Dickens's formulas in writing his novels was always that the heart had its reasons. Logic could not prevail.

Mrs. Sparsit, Bounderby's housekeeper, was eager to trap Louisa and James Harthouse in their love affair. This was but one example of her many unpleasant qualities, not the least of which was a dubious ancestry. Tracing the decline of her fortune, Dickens noted that Mrs. Sparsit had after all

> been a Powler—an ancient stock who could trace themselves so exceedingly far back that it was not surpris-

ing if they sometimes lost themselves—which they had rather frequently done—as respected horseflesh, blindhookey, Hebrew monetary transactions and the Insolvent Debtor's Court.[11]

In many ways, then, Dickens managed to align the aristocratic or upper middle class, for whom he had obviously little use, with those who were deep in fraudulent financial activities, presumably indulged in by Jews, together with likeminded, vulgar Bounderbys and myopic Gradgrinds.

It remained for Dickens to pit the whole business of creative life against the monetary values in *Little Dorrit*. It is by now a commonplace that the whole thrust of his novel flowed from Dickens's abhorrence of imprisonment for debt in England. It was of course irony compounded to realize that the book itself— the story of a father and his angelic daughter who ultimately were released from the Old Marshalsea through the endeavors of a benevolent soul—was written after the law for such imprisonment had been abolished. But Dickens was loath to forgo equating the stain of money with greedy commercialism. He had the luckless Dorrit entrust his rediscovered fortune to his in-law banker, Mr. Merdle, whose millions constricted and confined untold numbers of people. So, when Merdle committed suicide because of his speculations and swindles (much as Anthony Trollope's Melmotte would do later in the century in *The Way We Live Now*), his demise brought only confusion and desolation to thousands, and tightened the prison bars for debtors all over England. Could Merdle, who, ironically enough, escaped the prison that surely awaited him, have been a transformed Fagin, a Fagin grown large with power, a more devious character than that original poor thief of a Jew?

With *Our Mutual Friend*, Dickens's variations on the theme that love of money was the root of all evil became fully orchestrated. He peopled his novel with the nouveaux riches, whose greed knew no bounds. They preyed on each other and pursued wealth so meretriciously that they corrupted their own lives and whomever their lives touched. Dickens so caricatured the Lammles, the Veneerings, and the Podsnaps, with their crested tableware, their "corpulent straddling epergnes," their vulgar dress, and their sharp money deals, that they emerge as grotesques of the well-to-do in the Anglo-Jewish community of Victorian England.

> They were [Mr. Lammle's] friends...[and] between the room and the men there were strong resemblances. Both were too gaudy, too slangy, too odorous of cigars and too much given to horseflesh...[Recall Mrs. Sparsit's ancestry:][The room's decorations] of high stepping horses seemed necessary to all of Lammle's friends—as necessary as their transaction of business together in a gypsy way at untimely hours of the morning and evening in rushes and snatches. There were friends who seemed to be always coming and going across the Channel on errands about the Bourse and Greek and Spanish and Indian and Mexican and par and premium and discount and three-quarters and seven-eighths. They were all feverish, boastful and indefinably loose; and they all ate and drank a great deal; and made bets in eating and drinking. They all spoke of sums of money to be understood....They seemed to divide the world into two classes of people: people who were making enormous fortunes and people who were being enormously ruined. They were always in a hurry and yet seemed to have nothing tangible to do, except a few of them (those mostly asthmatic and thick-lipped who were forever demonstrating to the rest with gold pencil cases which they could hardly hold because of the big rings on their forefingers), how money was to be made.[12]

Was Dickens himself then overtly anti-Semitic because he associated the pursuit of money with Jews or those who resembled Jews? This question would appear to be irrelevant in the light of Dickens's own origins. Though his parents were Church of England people, Dickens was rooted in that kind of Protestant Christianity which in the Calvinist tradition, saw nothing wrong with the prudent money-gathering and money-keeping endeavors of hard-working, honest tradesmen, but which looked with jaundiced eye at activities that bore the slightest resemblance to investments on an international scale. We remember that Defoe, in the century preceding Dickens, also objected to the international uses to which wealth would have been put, practices favored by the government, the Anglican Establishment, and the Jews who had returned to England on Cromwell's invitation. But Dickens himself had come from the lower middle class. While he may have laughed many of their pieties to scorn, thinking of these as so much "cant and humbug" in his novels, in his view of the sins of materialism he was still one with the Evangelicals. This orientation to life not only saw evil in the calculated uses of money for international ends, but connected such alleged evil with factual, or legalistic, interpretations of existence. This approach also stressed the passive acceptance of Christian grace as a means toward salvation, while it disdained an outwardly organized battle against evil. Such an attitude was basically non-Jewish in its makeup. The innocent heroes of Dickens's novels were the recipients of grace. They were victorious through no efforts of their own. His villains were further variations of the devil, Fagin, who measured their success in fiscal terms. Such practices would have been deemed heretical in an idealized Christian state, and to the degree that Dickens himself abjured such activities, to that degree was he a true Christian; he could scarcely have had any understanding of, much less a concern with a Jewish comprehension of evil. Whether such indifference would constitute outright anti-Semitism would be questionable.

Dickens had sold his home, Tavistock House, to a well-to-do Jewish matron. She was so chagrined at Dickens's portrayal of Fagin that he at last made amends, not only by a personal contribution to a well-known Anglo-Jewish charity, but also by fashioning a benevolent Jew, Mr. Riah, for *Our Mutual Friend*. This paragon of virtue was completely unbelievable. His goodness prevented him from acting a moneylender, although he was forced to serve as a front for a Christian usurer, Fascination Fledgeby. In addition, Riah provided a refuge for a poor Christian girl, Jenny Wren, so that she could make dolls' dresses for a living. Dickens was sufficiently perceptive to have framed Riah's observation that whenever one Jew sinned, the misdeed would be attributed to the entire race.[13] Apparently, Dickens felt that he had compensated for his creation of Fagin by fashioning Mr. Riah. What mattered, however, was that he still associated Jews with wealth, and wealth bore multiple negative connotations for him. He had taken Carlyle's view of the cash-nexus quite literally and was in agreement with Matthew Arnold, who expanded the accepted definitions of Philistines as heathen wanderers, unfeeling enemies, people content with parochial, legalistic cultures, and as complacent individuals satisfied with what was deemed an inferior sort of wisdom to include aggregations of persons obsessed with wealth and riches.[14]

To the sins of the wealthy, Dickens would have added the vice of dandyism. James Harthouse of *Hard Times* was a caricature of that dandy who helped shape England's destiny, Benjamin Disraeli. In introducing James Harthouse, who had come from London with letters of reference from Gradgrind to Bounderby, Dickens managed to include some oblique references to Disraeli's career as a diplomat and novelist. Dickens implied that new recruits among the Gradgrindians now include fine young gentlemen. These served as models, whom the Gradgrindians imitated by

> yaw-yawing in their speech like them and serving out with an enervated air and little mouldy rations of their economy on which they regaled their disciples.

Dickens observed that James Harthouse was a brother to one of those fine gentlemen. Harthouse himself, accordingly,

> had tried life as a Cornet of Dragoons and found it a bore; and had afterwards tried it in a train of an English minister

abroad and found it a bore, and had then strolled to Jerusalem, and got bored there.[15]

For humor, satire, and downright pique, Dickens managed to roll Disraeli and the latter's Levant-bound hero, Tancred, all into one.

Fascination Fledgeby, the unadulterated villain of *Our Mutual Friend*, also looked and acted the dandy with his effete airs and modish dress.[16] Dickens had nothing but scorn for the fop with his world-weary attitude, his boredom, and his dilletantism in every area of life from religion to science and art. What Dickens truly seemed to fear most were the consequences to England once such a gallant and his confrères were to take over the reins of government. For how could one whose lower-class origin and growing up included a year of humiliation as a twelve-year old in a blacking factory have regarded aristocrats as Disraeli did— as the future hope for a rejuvenated England?

Dickens could not have made his ridicule of the aristocratic class more apparent than in chapter 12 of *Bleak House*, where he described the social life of Chesney Wold, the baronial home of Lord and Lady Dedlock. Not only were the Dedlocks locked in, in a personal sense, to the obfuscatory legalism of long-delayed suits in Chancery, but they were also bound publicly to the uselessness of a political system where choice of leadership consisted of hopeless alternatives among incompetents. Though the satire was blunt edged, its point was sharp.

> Then there is my Lord Boodle of considerable reputation with his party, who has known what office is, and who tells Sir Leicester Dedlock with much gravity after dinner, that he really does not see to what the present age is tending. A debate is not what a debate used to be; even a Cabinet is not what it formerly was. He proceeded with astonishment that supposing the present government be overthrown, the limited choice of the Crown, in the formation of the new ministry, would lie between Lord Coodle and Sir Thomas

Doodle—supposing it to be impossible for the Duke of Foodle to act with Goodle, which may be assumed to be the case in consequence of the breach arising out of that affair with Hoodle; then giving Commons to Goodle, the Exchequer to Koodle, the colonies to Loodle, and the Foreign Office to Moodle, what do you do with Noodle? You can't offer him a presidency of the Council; that is reserved for Poodle. You can't put him in the Woods and Forest, that is hardly good enough for Quoodle. What follows? That the country is shipwrecked, lost and gone to pieces...because you can't provide for Noodle.[17]

Dickens's objections to inept aristocrats leading England out of its political and economic morass were, of course, compounded by the Disraeli mystique which, almost like a variation on that old Puritan theme, saw England as the new righteous Israel. Dickens was far too insular to have failed to recognize the basically alien origins of this notion. He would have had no use for Disraeli's Jewish Sidonia, who in *Coningsby* explained the vibrant, aristocratic ideal of a reawakened England, bound for new heights through the medium of inspired leaders, who would successfully forge bonds of unity between the propertied classes and the working people.

Both in *Coningsby* and *Tancred*, Disraeli, with his physical insistence on the superiority of the Jewish group, regarded his hero, Sidonia, as an exalted leader standing ready to impart the wisdom of the East to English leaders of government. It became Sidonia's duty, in purple prose, to revive England's hope in her time-honored institutions—the monarchy, Parliament, and the Anglican Church. The medium through which Disraeli's heroes were to make their influence felt was a curious amalgam of the best elements in Judaism and Christianity. Such unswerving faith reinforced Disraeli's belief in the sacredness of ancient Israel, a sanctity that he, in a disconcerting way, crudely united with racism.[18] One of his heroines, Eva, after acknowledging Christianity's Jewish roots, remarked to Tancred that

"We agree that half Christendom worship a Jewess and the other half a Jew, now let me ask you one question. Which do you think the superior race, the worshipped or the worshipper?"[19]

As matters turned out, Disraeli's superheroes left no permanent configurations in the literary portrait of the Jew. At best, his Alroys, Tancreds, and Sidonias were the recipients of that Disraeli obsession: since Judaism is the foundation stone for the edifice of Christianity and England is a Christian nation, its Jews deserve complete emancipation.[20] At worst, Disraeli's heroes lent themselves readily to caricature and black humor.

In his *Notes of a Journey from Cornhill to Grand Cairo*, Thackeray snickered at the seemingly outrageous religious customs indulged in by filthy East European Jews on their way to Jerusalem, and also ridiculed the American Consul to that city, Warder Cresson. Though he did not mention Cresson by name, it is obvious that Thackeray was also accusing him of falling prey to that charm of the great "Asian Mystery" which had so intrigued Disraeli and his literary heroes. In 1845, the very year of Thackeray's travels, Cresson had converted to Judaism. Thinking him insane, his family disowned him. But Cresson went to Jerusalem personally to await the coming of the Messiah.[21]

Posing as D. M. Shrewsbury, Thackeray included *Codlingsby* among his *Novels by Eminent Hands*. Here he parodied Disraeli and his work *Coningsby*. Disraeli was the member for Shrewsbury in Parliament in 1844, when *Codlingsby* was written. In his spoof, Thackeray allowed Godfrey de Bouillon, Marquis of Codlingsby, to fall madly in love with Miriam Mendoza, a bejeweled Jewess whose clothes alone were worth a fortune in diamonds. Her Renaissance apartment, hidden deep behind the unprepossessing façade of her family's London warehouse, contained priceless pictures, Aubusson rugs, and tapestries of incalculable value.

Her brother Rafael testified to their genuine quality. Overcome both by the elegance of the living quarters and the fair woman's rapturous singing, Codlingsby forgot to light his cigar. Thereupon, that plumed beauty carelessly picked up a 10,000 pound note lying on the piano top and lit his chibook. Miriam's wealth dazzled. But much more ominous were the oblique references Codlingsby overheard between Rafael and his agent. The two men hinted at a worldwide Jewish conspiracy to control the world through wealth; diplomats, kings, and the Pope himself were all privy to this intelligence.[22]

Anthony Trollope was more forthright than Thackeray in associating Jews with wealth and power, and putting that power at the disposal of Disraelian heroes. Like them, Ethelbert (Bertie) Stanhope of *Barchester Towers*, the ne'er-do-well son of an absentee clergyman, traveled to Palestine to find spiritual sustenance. There, he too met Sidonia. But this Sidonia was only a pallid creature compared to the original. He provided "no heaps of gold as large as lions," so that the "Judaized Ethelbert was again obliged to draw on the revenue of the Christian Church." Lack of funds then forced Ethelbert to abandon his new-found faith.

"Bertie" also owed much of his personality to Lady Bertie in Disraeli's *Tancred*. She too was continually in debt, and was forever yearning for the Holy Land, with its impenentrable "Asian Mystery." Like Trollope's Bertie, she also had monetary dealings with Sidonia.[23]

In another of Trollope's novels, *The Eustace Diamonds*, Mr. Emilius, the "Jew-preacher" and a convert to Anglicanism, was after Lizzie Eustace's wealth. A fop and a dandy, he was an obscene caricature of Disraeli himself. We recall that Disraeli, converted from his faith to Christianity, made his way into English society only after he married an M.P.'s widow, many years his senior. So too did Mr. Emilius follow the widowed Lady Eustace to Portray Castle, where he successfully sued for her hand. By the tale's end, we are informed that Emilius was an impostor, a Bohemian Jew from Prague, where he had abandoned his former wife.²⁴

Thackeray also lifted Disraeli's Lord Monmouth from *Coningsby* and transformed him into that aging Lothario, the Marquess of Steyne, who was Becky Sharp's lover in *Vanity Fair*. Both were older dandies, grown ugly and foolish in their pursuits of the pleasures of life, activities deemed unbecoming to them because of their advancing years. We recall that in eighteenth-century literature, age was no barrier to these beaux, who continued to lust after women in a most improper fashion.

But Disraeli had the last word in *Endymion*. There he turned Thackeray into an obnoxious journalist, St. Barbe, who denigrated all politicians, yet sought political favors for himself. Always to be bought by the highest bidder, he measured all activities in terms of their monetary value.

George Eliot would probably have denied that her *Daniel Deronda* bore any resemblance to Disraeli's racially inspired heroes. Deronda displayed none of the heroics attributed to Tancred or Sidonia. Eliot herself claimed that

> the fellowship of race to which Disraeli refers the munificence of Sidonia is so evidently an inferior impulse which must ultimately be superceded, that I wonder that even he, Jew as he is, dares to boast of it.

While Disraeli was bent on missionizing, to directing the world to justice based on Jewish notions of leadership, Eliot wanted only a reconstructed Zionist state, no better and no worse than other nation states. However, much as Eliot might have protested, a careful reading of *Daniel Deronda* shows that it does turn on its racial and biological qualities. Before she wrote *Daniel Deronda*, Eliot declared that "everything specifically Jewish is of low grade."²⁵ Precisely because she felt that way, she was able to comment on her pawnbroker, Ezra Cohen's, "vulgarity of soul." Though the Cohen family in London's East End was a physical link through which Mordecai was to impart his exalted notions of a restored Zion to Deronda, Eliot still wondered whether it was not "typical of Mordecai [as a Jew that his existence] was nested in the self-congratulating ignorant prosperity of the Cohens."[26] Here Eliot betrayed the same compulsion that affected Dickens and Thackeray: Jews were usually involved in some pejorative fashion with money.

Eliot's lack of perception in developing the Cohen-Deronda-Mordecai group of characters offered a profound contrast to her portrayal of the Christian couple in the novel. The motives and behavior of Gwendolen Harleth and her domineering husband, Grandcourt, remained startlingly clear. But the Jewish characters were only talking puppets for the philosophy Eliot expounded. Political rationalizations for creating a Jewish state did not justify any artistic demands that Daniel Deronda be linked to the Gwendolen Harleth story. Gwendolen might just as well have had a noble, true-born Christian teach her the lessons of sacrifice and humility in the face of adversity brought on by her own wilfullness. But Deronda, that startlingly passive vessel of a reborn Zion, became Gwendolen's mentor. Why then, for that role, did Eliot choose a Christian who only later discovered his Jewish origins? Some of the more immediate responses might be that she and George Henry Lewes, with whom she had decided to spend the rest of her life, had become friendly with Emanuel Deutsch, a famous Orientalist and Talmudic scholar, or that Lewes, as a member of a club devoted to studying the works of Spinoza, had met a brilliant Jew who became the prototype for Mordecai. A more satisfactory solution to the question of her choice of a Christian turned Jew would simply have been that, until she wrote *Daniel Deronda*, Eliot's earlier novels derived their tension from the forces that existed between her characters and the communities in which they lived. But her own style of life and her rejection of orthodox Christianity had cut her off from her own community. She thereupon replaced her traditional faith with the belief that the ideal of goodness was equivalent to the idea of God. The purpose of Daniel Deronda, then, was to apply the force of such goodness to Gwendolen Harleth, who ultimately realized the evil effects of her capriciousness. Daniel Deronda might also have been Eliot's choice as Gwendolen's teacher because, like the author, he too had been cut off from his own true community.[27]

George Eliot herself was intent upon viewing *Daniel Deronda* as a unified work. To the degree that Deronda was the active agent toward beneficent ends for the Gwendolen Harleth section of the book and the passive agent for the goodness Mordecai sought in the second volume, she was correct. But it would seem that Eliot's traditional view of Jews as being "low grade" militated against the complete literary development of her Jewish characters. Throughout, Mordecai was never fully fashioned. At best, he emerges as a voice, while Deronda, either as Gwendolen's lay confessor or as Mordecai's messenger, never seems to have a life of his own. The details that went into re-creating the life of the Jewish pawnbroker's family, the Cohens, or that limned the eccentricities of the German-Jewish musician, Herr Klesmer, and that enlarged on the sweetness of the Jewish heroine, Mirah, are amazing in the wealth of knowledge they reveal. But at the same time, Mirah was sweet to the point of improbability; Klesmer's peculiarities resolved themselves into a heavy-handed humor, and, as noted before, in depicting the Cohens, George Eliot was unable to refrain from making that habitual association of Jews with money.

Anthony Trollope's *The Way We Live Now* appeared one year before *Daniel Deronda*. But what had been described as Cohen's "vulgarity of soul" or "amiable self satisfaction," had in the Trollope work been expanded to include the view of the Jew as the wealthy capitalist fraud, the chief swindler in money matters on whom lesser parties of all stripes in Victorian society thrived. The only decent Christian in the lot, though still an anti-Semite, Roger Carbury, warned his cousin, Lady Matilda, against the nefarious Melmotte. That odious millionaire, suspected of being of Jewish origin, was regarded

> as an adventurer and a swindler. No one pretends to think he is a gentleman...he amasses his money not by honest trade, but by unknown tricks as does a card-sharper....we would not admit [him] into our kitchens, much less to our tables on the score of his own merits. But because he has learned the art of making money we...settle upon his carcass as so many birds of prey.[28]

By the time the story has run its course, all those who settled on Melmotte's carcass have been duped. His reputation for wealth amassed on the Continent was surety enough for him to float a fraudulent stock for a spurious railroad involved in a non-existent right-of-way from Salt Lake City to Vera Cruz in Mexico. During his ascent up the social ladder, Melmotte even entertained the Emperor of China and won a seat in the House of Commons from Westminster. But his financial peccadilloes, which finally turned on the issue of a forged document in the sale of an estate, proved too much even for him. This resulted in his dramatic death by his own hand.

Two other Jewish associates of Melmotte, Cohenlupe, a sneak, who was the M.P. for Staines, and Ezekiel Breghert, a fat, greasy-faced millionaire of fifty, physically repulsive though not the charlatan that Melmotte was, helped round out Trollope's view of Jews. But if the Jews were vile, his Christians were not much better; the sharply honed edge of Trollope's cynicism laid bare the ways in which all these cheats gulled each other. In one subplot Breghert had the satisfaction of reneging on his engagement to Georgiana Longestaffe, a spinster who indulged in anti-Semitic notions, while she yet looked forward to a life of comfort as a married woman in which she would pass her husband off as a Christian by having him attend church on Sundays. To compound the irony, after Melmotte' death her father was forced to work closely with Breghert in rendering a true account of Melmotte's debts.

The other theme in this story, that of Marie Melmotte and Sir Felix Carbury, is also spun on money to lend gusto to the shallowness of the lovers' emotion. A true descendent of Jessica, Marie was perfectly willing to rob her father of his wealth and elope with Felix. Preparatory to the elopement, she stole a check from her father and reached Liverpool. But her Felix dallied and gambled away their fare to America. America.Having seen her groom in his true light, Marie finally married an American, Hamilton K. Fisker, the biggest scoundrel of them all, who, after having earlier tricked her fraudulent father, would now practice his chicanery on her. Her first suitor, Felix, at the instigation of her mother's lover, was banished to Germany, with an insufficient allowance for his gambling needs. Of all the ne'er-do-wells, only Paul Montague, Fisker's one-time partner and the recipient of Roger Carbury's solicitude, was able to extricate himself from the evil influences of greed and cupidity.

Despite satirical innuendos against the Jews, by dramatists, novelists, and versifiers, their social assimilation into Christian society intensified. In particular, close social contact between the English aristocracy and wealthy Anglo-Jewish families had been established as early as the previous century, and they flourished in the Victorian period. Moreover, at this time the political and civil emancipation of the Jews took its cue from rights awarded other religious minorities. In addition, the economic prosperity and social well-being of the Jews now paralleled the industrial, technological, and demographic growth of the nation as a whole. In terms of the Anglo-Jewish community, occupations became more diversified. Jews expanded their financial activities beyond merchant banking and began to enter the medical and legal professions in increasing numbers. The number of Jews in middle-class vocations grew: textile manufacturing, the china and glass industry, clothing, shoes, and the furniture trade attracted Jewish entrepreneurs. There was also a decrease in that old vocation so dear to the Jewish poor, street hawking and dealing in old clothes. Many Jews had crossed the poverty line and reached the middle class.

Yet affluence guaranteed no such overwhelming beneficent portrait of the Jew in literature as to wear out any basic concept of the Jew. Thomas Babington Macaulay and William Hazlitt may have been stirred by justice to demand the removal of civil disabilities for Jews. Byron's echoes of romantic yearnings about an outcast people may have struck some responsive chords. But the dominant note of the century was still Dickens's, Thackeray's, and Trollope's jaundiced view of Jews warped by wealth.

For some of the major novelists of the nineteenth century then, all Jews from Fagin to Melmotte were tainted by dint of their association with money. The evils flowing from this money relationship spread out their tentacles to crush all, Jew and non-Jew alike. On other occasions, however, when Disraeli's own heritage and cultural antecedents or Eliot's vast intellectual prowess expressed aspects of Jewish interests other than the bête noire of the cash-nexus, those qualities found their rationale in the belief in Jewish separateness, in Jewish uniqueness and, at times, even in Jewish racism.

Racist obsession became one of the more widespread currents of thought in the last third of the nineteenth century. Its implications led to theories of inferior and superior peoples, to divisiveness between the seeming rootedness of settled Christians with traditional values, and the alleged rootless cosmopolitanism of Jews with radical ideas. Anti-alien attitudes toward the Jews became expressions of the popular will. Implicit theories of race were given added dimension by using names symbolically to denote mental or physical attributes. Melmotte, involved in financial swindles in France and on the Continent really means "evil word" in French; Breghert represented a braggart, while Cohenlupe connoted

Jewish origin by the term *Cohen*, and *lupe* stood for *wolf*. Even little Jacob Cohen, the pawnbroker's son in *Daniel Deronda*, spoke with a voice "hoarse in its glibness as if it belonged to an aged commercial soul fatigued with bargaining through many generations."[29] In the same spirit, Mr. Emilius' "greasy hair" "hooky" nose and "disagreeable squint" in one eye seemed to lend credibility to his scheming "hypocrisy" and his "craving" for Lady Eustace's money.

Toward the very end of the century, racism in its ugliest manifestations found expression in the cheap sensationalism of George du Maurier; in his *Trilby* the horrors inspired by the earliest images of the Wandering Jew legend were foisted on the villainous and obscene Svengali, who hypnotized Trilby into becoming an accomplished singer.[30]

During the last two decades of the nineteenth century, thousands of Jews, fleeing renewed religious and economic persecution in the Russian Empire, arrived on the English scene. Their presence intensified some of the literary tendencies already alluded to. There were now more portrayals of capitalist Jews as international swindlers, along with increased attempts to deal with the distinctiveness of Jewish patterns of living. These patterns usually were pitted against a Christianized Western orientation to life. Frequently, in this counterplay between what amounted to two different value systems, the old bugaboo of the cash-nexus relationship was once again seen to dominate the life of the Jewish participants. And on those occasion where intermarriage was involved, both sets of parents now tended to voice their objections on racial rather than religious grounds. What seemed new in British writing at that time was not only that the arrival of the Jews produced an increase in the number of Old Testament and biblical romances, but that the Jews themselves, chief aong them Israel Zangwill, tried to portray the newcomers as fully rounded figures, realistic human beings, in whom the conflict between the insulated, traditional life of the East European ghetto, which constituted a religious civilization all its own, was weighed against the secular materialism of a free English society.[31] But this is a topic that properly belongs in a study of Jewish writers.

It has indeed been fashionable to describe the Victorians as torn between the effects of poverty and prosperity, between doubt and affirmation, between a recourse to man's rational impulses and a realization of his intuitive spiritual potential. While Matthew Arnold emerged as the great mediator in this battle between belief and incredulity and would have made a religion out of culture, Robert Browning, alone of the Victorians, saw life whole. His poetry burst forth as a welcome change from the novelists' obsession with guilt brought on by wealth, an obsession that frequently made the Jew the symbol of all that was wrong with society. But because Browning's was the vision of the integrated life, he harbored no prejudices. He sketched his people with as deliberate a psychological fidelity as he limned his villains. The anonymous monk who castigated Brother Lawrence in *The Soliloquy of the Spanish Cloister* seemed all the more human because of his mindless jealousy. The Duke of Ferrara may never have revealed the precise fate that his commands brought upon his wife in *My Last Duchess*, but his blatant materialism made him all the more comprehensible to the reader, while the worldiness of the mordant bishop in *The Bishop Orders His Tomb at St. Praxed's Church*, lent verisimilitude to that old man's machinations at the very edge of the grave.

Browning's ability to view his poetic characters as three-dimensional flesh-and-blood people is also observable in his *Rabbi Ben Ezra*, the Jewish sage from medieval Spain, on whom Browning willingly foisted so much of his own philosophy. *Rabbi Ben Ezra* expands upon a theme that Browning had resorted to in one of his earlier works, *Paracelsus*— that the essence of existence is found in man's striving for good, in his perfectibility. The effort itself was of greater consequence than the good to be achieved. And in

Rabbi Ben Ezra Browning acknowledged that the spiritual doubt the Rabbi felt as a young man was itself worthy for it partook of the divine ability to question. As spiritual struggle was proper to youth, so now in old age would the Rabbi be obligated to seek and know God. And by knowing the Infinite, the old man would realize that much of what had been part of his make-up had been hidden from his companions here on earth. Only God, as a potter who fashions mortal clay on his wheel, would know what was completely engraved on the soul, while man, in turn, would partake of the meaning of God. Such knowledge would grant the Rabbi the fortitude to overcome all obstacles in life's path, to look on old age as the fulfillment of the pattern of existence, and to welcome death as still another challenge with the end not yet in sight.

It would be a happy view that those qualities of his own which Browning ascribed to Ben Ezra truly characterized that medieval Hebrew philologist, poet, and biblical exegete. It would also force the issue to say that Browning's own views of the divine purpose in life, or of the eternal battle between evil and ever-victorious good, were Hebraic in origin. More accurate would be the observation that Browning had sympathetic ties with Jews and Hebraic culture. He probably was able to read the Bible in the original; some of his poems reveal an accurate knowledge of Hebraic lore. In *The Ring and the Book* he was aware of the extent of Christian religious bigotry against the Jews and made one aspect of that bigotry the subject of one of his "ironic monologues", *Holy-Cross Day*. His *Jochanan Hakkadosh* is the story of a rabbi whose life was prolonged by having each of his four disciples contribute three months of their own lives. But the rabbi's "mystic" ability to comprehend life came to him only because of the "accidental gift of three months of a child's life." In *Filippo Baldinucci on the Privilege of Burial*, Browning spoke up for the Jew's right to honorable burial, even though it involved deluding a Christian. On another occasion he expanded on a text from a Hebrew ethical treatise, *The Sayings of the Fathers*. In all of these literary creations, Browning's vast erudition, tempered by his humanism and compassion, was evident. The realistic qualities of his poems are heightened by his frequent recourse to dramatic monologues, to a harsh, often truncated phraseology, and to sudden shifts in thought or expression. His fidelity to psychological realism did not detract from his abiding optimism that ultimately all was for the best in this world. God, after all was in His heaven, and all was right.[32]

6
Alienation and the Cult of the Individual

THE certitude that had been part of Browning's life reinforced his cheerful eagerness. Yet in the midst of all that pleasant ambience, the earlier frustrations and conflicts of the Victorian Age grew into the nativisms and doubts of the twentieth century. Scientific skepticism and an emphasis on empiricism helped erode individual morality, which had been based on accepted social values. In the political arena, imperialism, which had once engendered a sense of pride in England's customs and institutions, came to be regarded as a system of induced slavery. Economically, living standards improved for British workers because of the increased power of the Labor Movement. However, unionization alone was not the key to a happier, more meaningful existence for everyone. To compound the difficulty, a belief in the classless society as the ideal state did little to secure man's goals or purposes in life. Similarly, substituting the group for the individual did not solve private moral dilemmas. Socialism may well have been the herald of the new age, and scientific determinism was quite prepared to plot human behavior both for the present and for the future. Unfortunately, such attempts at interpreting the modern condition did little to reassert man's significance in the world or to clarify his goals. The result in Britain was literature that reflected man's alienation from himself, from others, and from the many ideals that he had once held.

In keeping with this new sense of individualism, George Bernard Shaw revolted against sterile plodding nineteenth-century melodrama. He declared that he would let his characters "rip," that the flow of ideas and action in which they engaged would form a natural, if sometimes illogical order of events. Such a policy produced slightly mad sets of human beings who peopled his plays. In *Man and Superman* it was the Jewish brigand, Mendoza, transformed as devil in a dream sequence, against whom the hero, Jack Tanner, agrued his case. He protested that truth, beauty, and justice, which properly belong in hell, made that place all the more boring. Shaw had grafted his own reversal of values onto the medieval tradition of the Jew as devil. He was still the fiend, though only in a dream, and he bore a stereotypical Jewish surname, "Mendoza." Were all the virtues to be consigned to Hades, the Jew would become their proper guardian.

In this journey on the road to rebellion, Shaw also modified the usual association of Jews with wealth. In *Major Barbara* the Jew, Lazarus, was the silent partner in Andrew Undershaft's million-dollar munitions plant. But while Undershaft and Lazarus were prepared, like Barabas of old, to make war for the sake of profits, the rationale for their course of action had changed. Undershaft was convinced that poverty is worse than death. Therefore he and Lazarus had to foster wars everywhere to insure a continuous demand for their military hardware. Only in this way could they have guaranteed their factory workers the benefits of full employment. Even Major Barbara, Undershaft's evangelist daughter, knuckled under to the lure of her father's and Lazarus's millions: like the miser's gold of long ago, such wealth would breed, growing in direct proportion to increases in casualties and deaths on the battlefield. And by the time the play had run its course, Barbara would have no scruples about using ill-gotten gains for religious and charitable purposes.

Shaw's satire cut deep. Its very outrageousness proclaimed its Swiftean quality. But there were differences. Unlike Swift's, Shaw's irony did not dwell on the issue of Jews as a "stiff-neck'd people," a loathsome collectivity bound together to work its evil upon unsuspecting Anglicans. In fact, Shaw once admitted the superior wisdom of doing business with Jews and thought it advantageous, from a profit motive, to prefer their company to Christians.[1] The association of Jews with money-getting did not lead him to condemn them as a group. But by the time Shaw had completed destroying *all* the idols of his fellow human beings, he had come round to *Heartbreak House*. There all the values of Western civilization broke down; there men, ambiguous and contradictory, were separated from one another, and there, happiness, to be achieved by reaching the seventh degree of concentration into nothingness, was to be found in imbibing rum. In Shaw's literary world, then, the Jew was merely another characterization to be used for iconoclastic purposes. But even for Shaw, the literary image of the Jew still grew from the traditional Christian way in which he had earlier been perceived. Either he was the devil, or was associated, in however novel a fashion, with the accumulation of wealth.

Unlike Shaw, James Joyce did see his Jewish protagonist in ethnic terms. What was new, however, was that now the Jew's ethnicity and alienation were taken for granted by the author. He did not pass judgment on these aspects; he merely recorded the reactions they evoked in the Jew and in those about him. This he achieved by emphasizing the Israelite and Irish strains in the characters he shaped.[2]

James Joyce's *Ulysses*, one of the great masterpieces of twentieth-century literature, is a symbolic, naturalistic, poetic novel of man's eternal quest for identity. Here Joyce blended actual events and interior monologues in the lives of Leopold Bloom, an unprepossessing middle-class Jewish advertising salesman from Dublin, of his sexually adept singer-wife, Molly, and of Stephen Dedalus, a young Catholic teacher, to show how each of these people, within the same twenty-four-hour period of June 16, 1904, tried to learn to know himself.

For each, the acts engaged in on their journeys, both actual and metaphorical, were disarmingly simple, but like all simplicities they had profound implications whose depths derived both from the inner significance Joyce attached to them and from the parallels drawn to the wandering of the Homeric Ulysses. Thus, in the first third of the book, Stephen, like Telemachus of old, began by seeking his father, and finally, toward the end of the volume, met up with Bloom, a modern Ulysses, wise, yet foolish and devious; mediocre, yet perceptive and sensitive. In the search Telemachus-Stephen not only engaged in all those activities common to the human species, breathing, sleeping, eating, hearing, seeing, talking, eliminating, but he also fantasized, rebuked himself for his treatment of his dying mother, taught school, wrote incomplete verse, and mistrusted his friends, who, in their arrogant, patronizing ways also represented Penelope's suitors, who had finally to be defeated.

In the second third of the book, Bloom too began the day's activities inauspiciously. He fed the cat, brought his wife, Molly, breakfast in bed, read a note from his daughter, and delivered a message to his wife from her lover and concert manager, Blazes Boylan. He also went to the baths to prepare for his attendance at Paddy Dignam's funeral; he stopped at the newspaper office to sign a contract for placing an ad; he spoke with Mrs. Breen on O'Connell Bridge and wandered into different pubs where he thought of his wife's past and current lovers. He also waited at a maternity hospital for the birth his neighbor's, Mrs. Purefoy's, child. Finally, he rescued Stephen from a brothel after a street brawl with the police. But the significances of these routine activities were to be found in the preoccupation of his mind with images of his dead son, Rudy, and with his failure as a husband to Molly. He was tempted to reform her, physically and spiritually, much as Ulysses also sought to return to Penelope. All of Bloom's hells did not exactly parallel Ulysses', but that did not matter. Like Ulysses, Bloom too was an exile in an alien land, in the midst of those who refused to understand him.

For this reason, Joyce made his Everyman a converted Jew and fashioned Bloom precisely not as a Jew who would be distinguished by his own formal credal adherences, but rather as one who was not part of the ethnic majority and therefore remained alienated. Certainly, none of Bloom's formal acts ever proclaimed his original Jewishness. Throughout the work, his one distinguishing characteristic, his attachment to an orange grove in Palestine, spoke volumes for his nationalistic yearnings, but it did little to enlarge upon any specific non-Christian orientation to life that he may have had. On the contrary, he had eaten pork, and found some solace in hearing the mass, though in his mind he tended to deride the physical implications of Communion. Yet Christians in other literature were also prone to similar musings. Had not Browning's Renaissance bishop who ordered his tomb at St. Praxed's said as much, that lying there for centuries he would hear "the mutter of the mass" and "see God drunk and eaten all day long?" It was not Bloom's acceptance or rejection of any one or more Christian practices that set him apart from the lower middle classes among whom he lived. It was merely that all the others felt him to be different.

Throughout the book these differences arose in such a way as to emphasize the distinctiveness of race. This was a universal condition that Joyce caught and whose various facets he detailed in a multitude of situations. Thus Bloom was prepared to tell a sick joke at his own expense at Paddy Dignam's funeral, but was not allowed to conclude it.

Stephen's headmaster, Mr. Deasy, had indulged in silly rantings over Jewish control of the world. At the newspaper office, Bloom encountered some intellectual anti-Semites who associated Shakespeare's (spurious) Jewish origin with greed and uxoriousness. In the final meeting between Stephen and Bloom, the old blood-libel story, now seen as a variant of the Hugh of Lincoln legend, was sung. It was almost as though *The Prioresses Tale* had come full circle.

However, unlike his predecessors, similarly masters in the art of fiction, Joyce did not stoop to the caricaturized convention of the Jew, whose alleged evil was always to be associated with the immoral uses of wealth and vulgar taste. Joyce was not a Dickens, nor a Thackeray, nor a Trollope. But, first among the great novelists of the new age, he saw the Jew merely from the angle of an ethnic uniqueness, as one who was distinct from the rest of that society in whose midst he dwelled. With the possible exception of George Eliot, no British author had previously manifested such intuition or insight into the specifics of the Jewish psyche. Critics have seen resemblances between Joyce himself and Bloom, and it is true that Joyce laughed at himself. But that is inconsequential. What is important was that Joyce did not pass judgment on those differences which defined the Jew in popular terms. Instead, he merely recorded the emotional reactions of Bloom and his acquaintainces to each other.

Bloom's alienation was revealed in that scene at Barney Kiernan's Pub in Little Britain Street, where an unnamed citizen mocked the excesses to which Irish patriotism was prone. Like the one-eyed cannibalistic cyclops of old who threatened Ulysses, here the anonymous citizen, molded to gigantic proportions and accompanied by a ferocious dog, cursed Bloom in the elaborate mode of a Celtic epic. But he cursed him for the sheer pleasure of it, even when Bloom tried to reason with him or weigh all the issues of any problem. To the citizen's description of the rule of fearful autocracy in the British Navy, Bloom responded with

Alienation and the Cult of the Individual

"Isn't discipline the same anywhere? I mean wouldn't it be the same here if you pit force against force?"

But the citizen's reaction was violent.

"Didn't I tell you? As true as I'm drinking this porter, if he was at his last gasp, he'd try to downface you that living was dying."[3]

After the citizen, with the help of his confrères, had completed his catalogue of Irish martyrdoms at the hands of the English, the French, the Spaniards, and the Germans who had usurped the English throne, everyone "had a laugh at Bloom," for he did not fit his own description of a national as one who belongs to a nation "of the same people living in the same place."[4] While the others guffawed, the citizen spat at Bloom. Yet Bloom was not to be outdone. He identified himself as belonging to a race that was "Robbed . . . Plundered. Insulted. Persecuted." In his willful obtuseness, the citizen asked Bloom if he were talking about the new Jerusalem. Once Bloom answered, using the word, *love*, the citizen, deliberately misinterpreting Bloom's equation of love with life, called the Jew "a new apostle to the gentiles."[5]

This was a harsher treatment of Bloom than had occurred during the earlier episodes, at Paddy Dignam's funeral, or at the newspaper office where the editor swore at Bloom but did not threaten him. But the citizen's new and further level of degradation evoked a response from Bloom that appeared pathetic, courageous, and somewhat ludicrous all at the same time. Like Ulysses of old, Bloom, having shown his historic affiliation with his race, went on to shout

"......three cheers for Israel,"

as his friend Martin Cunningham tried to get him away from the citizen's shouted obscenities, or the crude advice of the shady narrator who ranted with

"Arrah, sit down on the Parliamentary side of your arse for Christ's sake and don't be making a public exhibition of yourself,"

along with other choice expressions contributed by

all the ragamuffins and sluts of the nation round the door.

Finally, Bloom managed to retort,

"Mendelssohn was a jew and Karl Marx and Mercandante and Spinoza. And the Saviour was a jew, his father was a jew. Your God."

To the rather bitterly humorous interpolation by the "good Christian, Martin"

"....he had no father,"

Bloom modified the answer by saying,

" . . .well, his uncle was a jew. . . your God was a jew, Christ was a jew like me."

These words put the citizen into such an apoplectic state that he swore,

"by Jesus, says he, I'll brain that bloody jew man for using the holy name. By Jesus, I'll crucify him, so I will. Give us that biscuit box there.[6]

The hilarity that such lines called forth was matched only by Joyce's parody of newspaper articles, which, describing the tin box's clattering after Bloom in his wagon, ultimately elevated that clatter to the level of an earthquake, an earthquake to which church and state responded, to their glory.

The catastrophe was terrific and instantaneous in its effect...there is no record extant of a similar seismic distur-

Alienation and the Cult of the Individual 135

bance in our island since the earthquake of 1534, the year of rebellion of Silken Thomas....all the lordly residences in the vicinity of the Palace of Justice were demolished and that noble edifice itself, in which at the time of the catastrophe, important legal debates were in progress, literally a mass of ruins beneath which it is to be feared all the occupants had to be buried alive.

Because the earthquake was accompanied by a cyclone, the headgear and the silk umbrella with its initialed gold head that bore the arms and house number of the Recorder of Ireland were discovered in other "remote parts" of the island. Expressions of sympathy poured in from all over the world.

> Messages of condolences are being hourly received from all parts of the different continents and the sovereign pontiff has been graciously pleased to decree that a special *missa de profunctis* shall be celebrated simultaneously by the ordinances of each and every church of all the episcopal dioceses subject to the authority of the Holy See in suffrage of the souls of those faithful departed who have been so unexpectedly called from our midst. The work of salvage, removal of debris, human remains, etc. has been entrusted to Messrs. Michael Meade and Son, 159 Great Brunswick Street, and Messrs. J.C. Martin, 77, 78, 79 and 80 North Wall, assisted by the men and officers of the Duke of Cornwall's Eighth Infantry under the general supervision of H.H.H. Rear Admiral, the Right Honorable Hercules Hannibal Habeas Corpus Anderson, K.E., K.P., P.C., C.K.B.,M.P., D.S.C., S.O.D., MF. H., MR. I.A., BL., MUS. DOC., P.L.G.,FT. C.D., F.R.U.I., F.R.C.P.I., and F.R.C.S.I.

Joyce then pricked the rhetoric of his own style by reminding the reader that the fight between the citizen and Bloom began over some misplaced horse bets. The last paragraph of the chapter reverts to a mock-heroic biblical tone and Bloom's escape from Kiernan's tavern is compared to Elijah's ascent to heaven, where the customers beheld

Him, even him, Ben Bloom, Elijah amid clouds of angels ascended to the glory of the brightness at an angle of 45 degrees over Donohoe's in Little Green Street like a shot off a shovel.[7]

If aspects of nationalism and faith set Bloom apart from others in Kiernan's Pub, then at the maternity hospital where he stopped to inquire after a neighbor, Mrs. Purefoy, he alone revealed a whole range of emotions alien to Stephen, to his friends, and to some of the medical students. Bloom was compassionate and humane, while the rest jested at fertility, childbirth, and the life giving process,[8] much as Ulysses' crew ate the divine oxen of the sun's pasture, for which their ship was destroyed by a thunderbolt and they were all killed.

In their biting jests at any affirmation of life, Stephen and his colleagues parodied all styles of language, from the biblical, to the hortatory Anglo-Saxon mode, to the medieval scholastic forms of writing and on to an imitation of the turgid prose of the seventeenth century metaphysicians. Through it all, the young men seemed to be saying that in the end all life winds down to a nothingness.

> ...the aged sisters draw us unto life: we wait, fatten, sport, clip, clasp, sunder, dwindle, dig over us dead they bend...and as no man knows the ubicity of his tumulus nor to what processes we shall thereby be ushered nor whether to a Tophet or to Edenville in like ways all hidden when we would backward see from what regions of remoteness the whatness of our wholeness hath fetched his whenceness.[9]

Joyce pitted Bloom against any such ascription of emptiness of meaning to life.[10] Bloom alone rejoiced that after a hard labor, Mrs. Purefoy gave birth to a boy. While the young men scored him in elegant eighteenth century clarity of language for his compassion, they also adverted to his

Alienation and the Cult of the Individual

alienism and commercial propensities, and added ugly innuendos concerning his own private sexual behavior.

> But with what pleasure let it be asked of the noble lord, his patron, has this alien, whom the concession of a gracious prince has admitted to civil rights constituted the lord paramount of our internal polity? Where is now that gratitude which loyalty would have counselled? During the recent war, whenever the enemy had a temporary advantage with his granados did this traitor to his kind not seize the moment to discharge his peace against the empire of which he is a tenant at will rather than tremble for the security of his 4%? Or is it that being a deluder of others, he has at last become his own and his only enjoyer? Far be it from candor to violate the bed chamber of a respectable lady, the daughter of a gallant major [Molly Bloom], or to cast the more distant reflection upon her virtue, but if he challenges attention there...then be it said so....But this new exponent of morals and healer of ills is at his best an exotic tree, which when rooted in its native orient grove and flourished and was abundant in balm, but transplanted to a clime more temperate, its roots have lost their quondam vigor while the stuff that comes away from it is stagnant, acid and inoperative.[11]

In a later episode, corresponding to the Homeric incident where Circe converted Ulysses' crew to swine, Bloom too, now completely dominated by his inner fantasies, viewed himself as a transvestite, eager to be debased, in a masochistic way, by the woman he had known, or was about to know, in a brothel. For having given a pig's trotter to a passing dog, he was arrested as a nuisance, and then was subjected to a Kafkaesque nightmare trial, in which his bankrupt attorney, J. J. O'Molloy, indulging in those stupidities of legal jargon which shape a form of black humor, pleaded Bloom's innocence of any sexual misconduct. He ascribed Bloom's guiltlessness either to his strange origin or to his insanity. Here, in a parody of a dramatic scene, O'Molloy spoke up in "pained protest":

> This is no place for indecent levity at the expense of an erring mortal disguised in liquor. We are not in a beergarden, nor at an Oxford Rag nor is this a travesty of justice. My client is an infant, a poor foreign immigrant who started scratch as a stowaway and is now trying to turn an honest penny. The trumped up misdemeanor which is due to a momentary aberration of heredity brought on by hallucination, such familiarities as the alleged guilty occurrences being...permitted in my client's native place, the land of the Pharaoh. *Prima facie*, I put it to you that there were no attempt at carnally knowing. Intimacy did not occur and the offense complained of Driscoll [Bloom's former maid servant] that her virtue was solicited, was not repeated. I would deal in especial with atavism. There have been cases of somnambulism in my client's family, of the accused, if the accused could speak, he could a tale unfold of one of the strangest that have ever been narrated between the covers of a book. He himself my Lord is a physical wreck from cholera's weak chest. His submission is that he is of Mongolian extraction and irresponsible for his action. Not all there in fact. . .
> By Hades, I will not have any client of mine gagged and badgered in this fashion by a pack of curs and laughing hyenas. The mosaic code has superceded to the law of the jungle . . . .when in doubt persecute Bloom.[12]

After the nightmare of the trial receded from Bloom's mind and the awaited execution was averted, he imagined himself the leader of the Irish people. Acting magnanimously on their behalf, he offered them a magical incantation of Hebrew letters of the alphabet, words meaning "phylacteries," "the sons of the covenent," "unleavened bread," "Germanic Jewry," and the term "insanity." Finally transformed into a Messiah, or Godhead, he was then pilloried in imitation of the Crucifixion.[13]

The net effect of such images, including the one where Bloom, transformed into a woman, gave birth to eight metallic children, all of whom became controllers of vast amounts of public wealth, strengthened the conventional caricature of the Jew as given to alien ways, immorality, arrogance, and lust for power. But in this instance, Joyce ascribed the fantasies to the victim himself; the Jew had come to believe what others were saying about him. Such negative connotations thereby lent themselves all the more easily to facile use by the Jew's detractors and calumniators, while they yet, by the very insanity of their argument, gave credence to those who would laugh such inanities to scorn. Joyce, by delineating the true inner reactions of Stephen, his friends, and the Irish populace to Bloom's very existence, and by portraying Bloom's own confused longing for love, security, and identity in what was a sterile Dublin wasteland, had made it possible to see Bloom, despite his alienation, as a veritable Ulysses, an Everyman who would endure.

In the light of Bloom's responses to those about him— he would affirm life while others mocked it; he would offer love while that unknown citizen in Kiernan's Pub counseled hate—there would be ample reason to agree with one critic that Bloom possessed Ulysses' classic temper, his heroic spirit.[14] In this sense, not only would Bloom persist, but he would also be aware of moral certainties in himself and others. Yet, after Bloom had rescued Stephen from the brothel, paid his bill there, comforted him after a cuff on the head by an exasperated soldier, talked with him in a cabman's shelter, and then finally engaged him in a long series of topics confined to the didactic logic and style of a catechism, there was communication, but little conscious understanding between the two men.

> What reduced to their simplest reciprocal form were Bloom's thoughts about Stephen's thoughts about Bloom and Bloom's thoughts about Stephen's thoughts about Bloom's thoughts about Stephen?
>
> He thought that he thought that he was a Jew, where as he knew that he knew that he knew that he was not.[15]

Put colloquially, when it came down to the nitty-gritty,

Bloom thought that Stephen thought that he (Bloom) was a Jew, while Stephen knew that he (Bloom) knew that he (Stephen) was not. Were this to be taken as literally as it sounds, the great gulf of separation between Stephen and Bloom had not been bridged.

Yet certain most-respected students of Joyce's *Ulysses* have insisted that Stephen, in his unconscious quest for love, charity, and compassion, found those qualities in Bloom (hadn't Bloom counseled love and pity for Mrs. Purefoy, and even for the "ragamuffins" in the pub?), and that Bloom, seeing in Stephen a new crystallization of his long-dead son, Rudy, was reintegrated once more, now to assert his rightful role as a husband to his unfaithful wife, Molly. It has also been suggested that Stephen, the young, rejected, and rejecting intellectual, sought not only his father, but also a justification for a creative reawakening of his literary talents, and that his temporary meeting with Bloom granted him that moment of clarification, a Joycean epiphany, which enabled him later to write his masterpiece, *Ulysses*.[16]

For those who would insist upon a spiritual basis for this novel, Stephen-Joyce-Telemachus would then be returning to his spiritual father, Ulysses-Bloom-God, and in the Christian sense, Christ, in whom all would merge and be one. To carry this analogy further, Stephen and Bloom, talking together in the cabman's shelter, participated in the rite of atonement (at-one-ment), partook of communion with Stephen drinking cocoa, the drink of the gods, while Bloom, in his kitchen, was both God and celebrant. Since by such consumption Stephen became one with God, he would be reinvested with creative-artistic powers. Stephen, then, to fulfill his mission, would have to leave the Father-God, in order to go off and forge the artistic reshaping of his race, its "uncreated conscience in the smithy of his soul."[17] Such a rendering would omit the Christian sacrifice of the Son; unless, of course, Stephen, as one with Bloom-God, fashioned-created with his word.

Like other modern writers, Joyce was fascinated more by

Alienation and the Cult of the Individual

the psychology than the structure of myths. Homeric parallels were able to provide suitable frames for Joyce's *Ulysses*, but while the Homeric Ulysses was of epic proportions, Bloom was not. It has been argued that it would be immaterial to wonder whether after the Stephen-Bloom meeting, Bloom's self-assertion, equated with Molly's giving him breakfast in bed, would be realized, or whether Molly in her long unfinished, two-thousand-word reverie would really revise her relationship with her husband. Most critics, with one exception,[18] have refused to consider the consequences of such uncertainties.[19] For them, the Stephen-Bloom meeting, temporary though it was, was sufficient to resolve the difficulties. Yet were Bloom of truly heroic proportions and Stephen a youth destined to grow to magnificence, the intent of Joyce's work would be diminished. Both Stephen and Bloom would have lost their human qualities, and the alienation in which Joyce fashioned them would lose its meaning. Was not Joyce essentially implying that Stephen and Bloom had come together once, only to drift apart again? But the "epiphany" of each, even so, would remain with them.

Ulysses, a novel that vibrates with the reality of human interactions, relationships that constitute the fabric of modern society, reveals both Stephen and Bloom as archetypes of twentieth-century man, lost, alienated, with few relevant values to replace the old certainties of home, nation, and faith. Perhaps Matthew Arnold, writing long before *Ulysses* appeared in print, expressed the true understanding of the Ulysses-Bloom, Telemechus-Stephen and Penelope-Molly story.

> Ah, love, let us be true
> to one another! for the world, which seems
> to lie before us like a land of dreams,
> so various, so beautiful, so new
> hath really neither joy, nor love, nor life
> nor certitude, nor peace, nor help for pain
> and we are here as on a darkling plain,

swept with confused alarms of struggle and flight
where ignorant armies clash by night.[20]

In *Ulysses*, James Joyce built a whole edifice on the tenuousness of human relationships made more fragile by the doubt cast forth in *Dover Beach*. It would also appear that Graham Greene reacted to the emptiness inherent in Arnold's warning by peopling his novelist's world with alienated characters. But whereas Joyce relied on interior thought and half-formulated, often paradoxical emotions to stress the uncertainty and aimlessness of his characters, Greene utilized authorial comments, involved plot sequences, and contrived coincidences to fashion people who, at the very end, were frequently brought to the brink of salvation through the proddings of the Catholic Church. Though a much younger man than Joyce, Greene was a master craftsman of that realistic type of writing which antedated Joyce. Greene produced novels, short stories, and dramas designed both to entertain and to instruct. Practically all of these works, whether shaped for didactic purposes or constructed as popular literary amusements, found their justification in Greene's Catholicism, which served either as an embellishment, or as itself constituting the religious allegory by which the tale could be resolved.

Such religious teachings frequently involved the Judas theme of betrayal, a motif whose application Greene intensified through an adept use of irony, particularly in *This Gun for Hire*, an "entertainment," as he called it, and in its sequel, *Brighton Rock*. James Raven, the betrayed hero of *This Gun for Hire*, was not a Christlike prototype, but a murderer and denizen of the underworld, whose passing Greene likened to that of the Christian Savior. In *Brighton Rock*, Pinkie Brown, the seventeen-year-old boy leader of a razor-wielding gang involved in the racetrack-protection racket, was evil incarnate. Yet, in forcing his young bride into a sham suicide pact so as to accomplish her murder, he forgot that it was her death, not his own, that he had intended:

Alienation and the Cult of the Individual 143

and looking out as if it was he who'd got to take some sort of farewell of the bike and the bungalow and the rainy street, he thought of the words in the Mass:

He was in the world and the world was made by Him and the world knew Him not.[21]

In both novels, the actual agents who betrayed the murderous nonheroes to the police were women, regarded either as representatives of humanity or as forces for natural justice. But, beyond the women, the very springs of evil themselves against whom Greene's rootless young men were pitted, were Jews.

This Gun for Hire is a swift, suspenseful thriller in which James Raven, a member of a gang involved, like Pinkie's, in the racetrack-protection frauds, was hired by one Cholmondeley (alias Davis, alias Davenant, and at odds with a seamy, mysterious, theatrical producer called Cohen), an agent of a wealthy Jewish steel mogul, Sir Marcus, to murder the humanitarian minister of a small European nation. Raven accomplishes his assignment, and the remainder of the novel consists of a double pursuit in which the police chase Raven, and Raven himself seeks Cholmondeley, his initial betrayer who had paid for the assassination in marked, stolen notes. But the heroine, Anne Crowder, fearful that the murder will lead to war, finally betrays Raven to her fiancé, Mather, the detective in charge of the case.

The ostensible purpose of the murder had indeed been political. Since the martyred minister had been an ardent advocate for peace, his death at English hands might have led to a confrontation between England and the unnamed European country whose representative he was, a state of affairs from which Sir Marcus, the wily Jewish director of Midland Steel, alone would benefit. Much like Andrew Undershaft of Undershaft and Lazarus in Shaw's play *Major Barbara*, Sir Marcus would secure enormous profits from any future battle. But whereas Shaw laughed up his sleeve when his Andrew Undershaft convinced his daughter that war was a desirable end because it insured wealth and prestige for the leaders while spurring employment for the population as a whole, Greene allows his Sir Marcus no humor whatsoever. For that alien, detestable creature, squatting over his millions much as T. S. Eliot's Jew squatted on his window-sill in contempt, was incapable, like Dickens's millionaire Mr. Merdle, of consuming any substantial food (for how could a devil eat as humans ate?). Greene's heroine, Anne Crowdor, recognized the malevolence of Sir Marcus and his tool, Cholmondeley, so that her first impulse was to agree with Raven in seeking the death of these malefactors. But simple justice demanded an awareness of Raven's own murderous deed. In the end Anne rationalizes her own betrayal of Raven to the authorities by convincing herself that his killing the minister would have made armed conflict inevitable.

Her disclosure of Raven's guilt compounds the irony of the final act before the police closed in on him. Moments before his imminent demise, he managed effectively to kill the villains of the piece and thereby evoke sympathy for himself, a sympathy heightened by reiterated descriptions of his appalling early childhood and adolescence. Greene, in fact, reached the very height of pity for the physically repulsive Raven, with his harelip and miserable eyes. Readers are informed that had Raven himself, as part of a poor, despised class, realized that the minister was a pacifist, he would not have agreed to the dastardly act. Further, Greene compares Raven with a scapegoat, one forced to suffer the evils of others. Had he not indeed, from one standpoint, suffered for the evils of Sir Marcus and Cholmondeley, even though he himself had originally been a willing partner in the enterprise?

By supplying these reasons for Raven's basically purposeless killing—a killing whose only real motive was the two-hundred pounds promised the penniless Raven—Greene cleverly mythologized his nonhero into a symbol of a universal sufferer. In his flight from justice, Raven reflected that "foxes have their holes, but the son of man...."[22] Raven's search for Cholmondeley and his attempts to elude the police occurred during the Christmas season in the Midlands industrial town of Nottwich. In his reaction to the reproductions of the Nativity scene in a storefront, Raven saw his own fate as Christ's, at the hands of a society that manipulated a legend out of an actual historic occurrence.

> They twisted everything, even the story in there, it was historical, it had happened, but they twisted it to their own purpose. They made him a god because they could feel fine about it all, they didn't have to consider themselves responsible for the raw deal they'd given him. He'd consented, hadn't he? That was the argument, because he could have called down "a legion of angels," if he'd wanted to escape hanging there. On your life he could, he thought, with better lack of faith, just as easily as his own father, taking the drop at Wandsworth [about to be hanged in prison], could have saved himself when the trap opened. He stood there with his face against the glass, waiting for somebody to deny that reasoning, staring at the swaddled child with a horrified tenderness—"the little bastard"—because he [Raven] was educated and he knew what the child was in for, the damned Jews and the double-crossing Judas, with no one ever to draw a knife in his side when the soldiers came for him.[23]

Christlike, then; and by the time Raven had Mather within sight of his automatic, he was unable to shoot. He

> couldn't work up any sourness, any bitterness at his betrayal...but he had been marked from his birth for this end, to be betrayed in turn by everyone until every avenue into life had been safely closed. . . .as he fixed his arm at the long reluctant last and Saunders [Mather's assistant] shot him in the back through the opening door, death came to him in the form of unbearable pain. It was if he had to deliver this pain as a woman delivers a child and he sobbed and moaned in the effort. At last it came out of him and he followed his only child into a vast desolation.[24]

For all the sympathy Greene garnered about him, James Raven plainly was not a Christian in the deepest meaning of the term. Only Pinkie Brown of *Brighton Rock* surpassed him in evil.

Pinkie was hard and his name seemed ineradicable, like the rock-candy manufactured in the seaside resort of Brighton, whose letters remained clearly imprinted even at the end of the sweet stick. *Brighton Rock* then became the story of Pinkie's criminal career. He was only a seventeen-year-old boy, yet he had inherited the leadership of a gang of crooks when its chief mobster, a criminal named Kite, was betrayed by a cheap journalist, Fred Hale, to a notorious Jewish gangster. This racketeer, Colleoni, was in league with the police. At Colleoni's request, James Raven, the Raven of *This Gun for Hire*, had first disposed of Kite before he proceeded to tackle that innocent, pacifist foreign minister.

Pinkie, as the new leader of Kite's mob, had to assert his independence and avenge his predecessor's murder. This he attempted to do by having his razor-wielding hooligans "carve up" Fred Hale. Though Hale died of natural causes just before he was to have been slashed, the intent of Pinkie and his cohorts had clearly been murder. Their motive might have remained hidden had it not been for Ida Arnold, a sleazy, voluptuous blonde of easy virtue, who had earlier taken a liking to Hale and suspected that he had been done away with. Ida, as the representative of decent society and eager to see justice done in its natural way, equated the whole matter with "an eye for an eye, a tooth for a tooth." She manages effectively, through a whole series of strange coincidences, to force Pinkie to his own death, when he, in turn, is almost about to succeed in persuading his young bride, Rose, into preceding him in "a sham suicide pact." To hide the fact that Hale had really been murdered, Pinkie had been forced to marry Rose. He wished now to dispose of her through her own self-destruction, for he regarded his wife as a threat to his virginity. He identified such chasteness with the purity of his religion and with his role as leader. But Ida Arnold, the stickler for what was right, had destroyed all that with her constant prying. In fact, Greene applied the measure of everyday morality to Ida's quest for truth so doggedly that her pursuit of righteousness became tedious. At last it grew horrible even for Rose, who was a symbol of Catholic goodness, and whose own search for theological certainty was fulfilled by an old priest who comforted her after Pinkie's death. After her confession that she had prepared to take her own life, he reassured her that it was better to live in sin an entire lifetime than to believe that any soul might suffer damnation in the afterlife.

On another occasion Greene had wondered why there had been such a to-do about *Brighton Rock*, for all he had written was the story of one man's journey to hell,[25] but its implications reach far beyond Pinkie's descent into the netherworld. On his way he gathers sympathy from author and reader and Rose, who though her intended suicide would have placed her in "mortal sin", did not want Pinkie to face the darkness by himself.[26] The priest's blessing could also extend posthumously to Pinkie; did not divine mercy include the damned? Only the Jewish gangster is so evil in mind and spirit, that having no compassion he cannot even reach into Pinkie's hell. And while Colleoni has that satisfying glow about him like one who controls "Parliament...cash registers . . . policemen and prostitutes,"[27] it is Ida, stalking justice, who manages to separate Rose from Pinkie, when all along as good and evil "they should have remained together."[28]

Why Pinkie merited God's forgiveness but Colleoni and Ida did not is beyond explanation. Equally mystifying is the fact that the priest's word would provide scant consolation for Rose. Returning to her room, she would find that record Pinkie had once made for her at a cheap shop in Brighton, a record which she had hidden in a cupboard and to which she would now listen. She would shortly discover "the horror of it all" in the words of her dead husband: "God damn you,

you little bitch, why can't you go back home for ever and let me be?"[29] What is clear however is that Greene's villainous protagonists are miraculously transformed by death, while the evil forces that sometimes join them or are at odds with them, the Jews and their followers, Colleoni of *Brighton Rock* and Sir Marcus of *This Gun for Hire* are never redeemed.

It would be simple enough to explain Greene's predilection for stereotyped Jewish villains—in *Orient Express*, it had been two merchant Jews, in *This Gun for Hire* and *Brighton Rock*, an armanents king and mobster—who served as modern day evidences of old anti-Semitic biases. Far more troublesome, however, would be the observation that Jews, or their unwitting representatives, had a part in doing Greene's evil geniuses to death. There has been a considerable amount of literary concern over Greene's fascination with his own morally and or physically repulsive fictive creations. Explanations with regard to his Manichaean or Jansenist tendencies have not been found wanting.[30] Yet the key question with regard to Greene's betrayed evildoers has not been asked. Were the Jews, or sometimes unwilling partners like Anne Crowder of *This Gun for Hire* or Ida Arnold of *Brighton Rock*, themselves the means by which divine justice was brought to bear, or were they still the emissaries of the devil?

Such queries would not be applicable to Evelyn Waugh's characterizations of Jews in his novels. These portrayals were merely extensions of stereotypes by earlier writers. This is all the more amazing in that Waugh's surrealist stories were mainly repetitions of one Shavian theme, the downfall of Western civilization with its humanistic values. In his madcap universe, his protagonists bordered on the comic, the satiric, and the insane. Yet his Jews were still cast in the old mold. In *Decline and Fall* Dr. Augustus Fagan, the headmaster of Llanabba Castle, a public school in Wales, was a swindler. The scheming Jesuit priest of *Vile Bodies*, Father Rothschild

S.J., was a fraudulent Jew, privy to the confidences of a Prime Minister. In *Helena* the Wandering Jew was prepared to sell religion as a useful commodity, and in *Men at Arms* even the Jewish refugees in Yugoslavia in World War II were cheats and hypocrites, involved in questionable trade arrangements, who did the Partisans out of what was rightfully theirs.

W. Somerset Maugham was also content to evoke the old ghosts of anti-Semitism. His Jews, or those approximating them, remained pushy and always on the edge of society, where they never quite made it. Elliott Templeton, of *The Razor's Edge*, despised a brash young Jew for engaging in questionable deals in art and antiques, the very sort of chicanery that was Templeton's own stock-in-trade. And almost to a man, the fellow passengers aboard ship in the story, "Mr. Know-All," of *Cosmopolitans*, disliked Max Kalada, who, Jewish or not, was plainly depicted as the stereotype of the Jewish fixer.

Anti-Semitism in John Galsworthy's play *Loyalties* is based on totally different premises than those of the works of Maugham and Waugh. Written in 1922, not long after the period when Joyce was experimenting with his rootless individuals but before Greene had commenced his fascination with seedy, isolated people on the fringes of society, *Loyalties* was a drama that dealt neither with murderous heroes, nor with ambivalent, quixotic, erratic personalities. Instead, its protagonists were typical representatives of Britain's upper and middle classes who put a premium on place and position in society.

The theme of this play was simple enough: except for rare occasions, most people placed group, class, religious, and ethnic loyalties to one another above moral considerations. To protect the reputation of any member of a specific clique was paramount. Under such circumstances silence and falsehood were to be fostered as part of a discreet, if somewhat subverted sense of honor.

In this story, a status-seeking young Jew, Ferdinand De Levis, who won almost one thousand pounds at the races by entering a filly for whose keep he had paid, then had those monies stolen from him by the animal's original owner. That was Ronald Dancy, a typical upper-class officer, who, together with his friends, frequented assorted racing and social clubs. Dancy and his peers lived by the gentleman's code of English society, which demanded loyalty at the price of honesty. The drama itself involved opening trial negotiations instituted by De Levis, where circumstantial evidence had already emphasized the likelihood of Dancy's guilt. That guilt was later corroborated through the intervention of two representatives of the middle classes, one of whom was an Italian, a rather recent immigrant to England.

As an officer in Britain's colonial forces and a military adventurer, Dancy strongly believed in the superiority of the English mind and temperament. This would partially explain why he saw nothing wrong in using the stolen money to pay off a "debt of honor" to the daughter of that Italian immigrant. This payment then released Dancy from any claims of affection she might have had upon him and allowed him to marry a woman of his own class. To Dancy such a transaction appeared as legitimate as robbing the Jew in the first place, the more so since the racing animal originally belonged to him. By the time the drama reached its denouement, De Levis, unlike Shylock, did not demand his pound of flesh. He only wanted justice done, and was prepared to donate his recovered purloined funds to charity. For his part, Dancy, still convinced of the morality of the gentleman's code of behavior, refused to accept his solicitor's suggestion or that of one of his John Bullish friends that he either go off to fight in Morocco, or through diplomatic contacts seek a position at the Spanish War Office. Instead, as his wife tried to postpone the moment of her husband's arrest, Dancy, in the bedroom, fired a bullet through his heart.

Throughout his ordeal, Dancy's friends remained loyal to him, even though they were aware of his guilt. Their common bond of anti-Semitism provided the justification for their action. To begin with, Charles Winsor, the owner of the country house where the theft occurred, and his wife, Lady Adela, implied that De Levis's wealth was ill-gotten and that he was thoroughly disliked both for his flashy ways and for having entered into a wager over some parlor trick with Dancy. Winsor and Lady Adela saw nothing wrong in Dancy's accepting the silly bet, but were still annoyed at De Levis's stupidities, such as his hankering after social status. After De Levis had openly accused Dancy of the theft, Dancy's colleagues banded together to blackball De Levis's admission to the latest in a series of social clubs. The only basis for his acceptance would have been a common decision on the part of all concerned to keep the matter of the robbery quiet. But since De Levis was both practical and astute enough to realize that he was tolerated only for his wealth, once that was gone the only recourse he had left was to recoup his losses. In acting on this premise, De Levis had broken the gentleman's code of behavior. He bruited the notion of the theft about the clubrooms; he refused to duel with Dancy so as to settle the matter at swords' point, and remained impervious to Dancy's request. Dancy wanted De Levis to apologize to him in writing for having had the effrontery to impute thievery to a gentleman and an officer. De Levis's adamant opposition only intensified the animosity that Dancy's peers felt toward him, while they found excuses for Dancy's behavior in the notion that he craved excitement and wondered whether two jury men, who appeared to be Jews, would not be prejudiced against Dancy. A potent dislike of Jews had prompted a prosperous middle-class merchant, Mr. Gilman, to offer evidence on Dancy's behalf, evidence that ironically enough became Dancy's undoing. When Gilman turned to a law clerk, assisting Dancy's solicitor, and said

"I don't like—Ebrews. They work harder, they're more sober, they're honest and they're everywhere. I've nothing against them, but they get on so,"[31]

he was voicing a common British complaint.

Like Shaw, Galsworthy had also abjured the well-made play of French extraction. He earnestly believed that a successful play depended upon the presentation of fully integrated, wholly realized characters, whose thoughts, motives, and actions would then determine the natural unfolding of the narrative. But *Loyalties* did not measure up to such a standard. Its attempt to weigh the consequences of anti-Semitism in a starkly personal, highly dramatic way among believable human beings led instead to the emphasis on plot over personality. The figures who then emerged, Dancy as a typical British colonial, the British upper society women who viewed a trial as a much needed thrill in their otherwise boring lives, the liquor-drinking, bridge-playing club members, the immigrant with his artificial Italian accent, and even De Levis himself—all proved to be uninspiring creations who mouthed hackneyed statements. To Dancy's ugly but familiar epithet of "damn Jew" hurled at him, De Levis responded almost in kind. Using words that Disraeli in another context had once made famous, De Levis said:

"My race was old when you were all savages. I am proud to be a Jew."[32]

There was only one insightful moment in the play that relieved the commonplace quality of such lines. That was when Jacob Twisden, the solicitor, convinced at last of Dancy's guilt, refused to defend him any further. Though Twisden chose this course against the inclination of his heart and will, it was an option that proved that on rare occasions and under extreme duress, the law will win out over group loyalties. It would appear that the only one in this play who cherished such a victory was the dramatist himself, who in real life had had some legal training.

At one moment during the chase in *This Gun for Hire*, James Raven overheard two women discussing the merits of *Loyalties*. They commented on its profundity and noted how humane the author was and that he was also a prominent antivivisectionist. Greene's irony here could not have been more trenchant, for Greene himself was writing of rootless outcasts, while Galsworthy dealt with people whose very close ties to each other reinforced their prejudices.

Though he was a later contemporary of Shaw and Joyce, and much of his work preceded Greene's literary output, Galsworthy did not properly belong to that generation of writers concerned with the isolated individual. Shaw's Jew-devil, Mendoza, and Jack Tanner in the dream-sequence in *Man and Superman* may have spoken at cross-purposes; Leopold Bloom and Stephen Dedalus, when they finally met, may have answered each other in catechismal form, but they did not communicate. Anne Crowdor listened to James Raven while other thoughts were crowding her mind, and Pinkie Brown was prepared to subvert all of Rose's ideas because he bore no emotional relationship to her, but Dancy and De Levis found a means for communication in the shared antipathy they felt to one another.

An attempt has elsewhere been made to show that C. P. Snow, in his novel sequences called the *Strangers and Brothers* series, was also interested in the essential isolation of the individual in society, hence his all-inclusive title for most of his fiction. While men ought in reality to have been brothers, they were in essence only strangers to one another.[33] But such an interpretation would put an undue strain upon the whole thrust of Snow's work. Snow was always more concerned with personal and group interactions in their relationships to the use and abuse of power than he was with the unique individualities of the characters he created.

Though his novels were not autobiographical, Snow used his own *persona* or mask in the guise of one Lewis Eliot, who, like himself, was at home both in the world of the humanities and in science. In the *Strangers and Brothers* sequence, Snow managed effectively to fashion Eliot as his narrator. At the same time, through clever reminiscing and effective cross-referencing to new sets of circumstances in a variety of his novels, Snow also allowed Eliot to grow to maturity. Eliot's own dynamism then permitted him to move in various circles of society with comparative ease. A barrister by profession, he was also an academician at an anonymous Cambridge college. He had close ties with eminent scientists, classicists, historians, administrators, statesmen, and politicians in government. Each one of the novels in this series then deals with a multitude of moral problems refracted against Eliot. Inevitably, those problems arose when power was to be altered in some fashion in some school, group, family, corporate entity, or governmental institution. Frequently, these institutions were intended as microcosms of larger ruling units. The changes in power structure that went on in the cloistered college of a university bore implications for the administration of a country. The adoption, for example, of a radical nuclear policy by England in the fifties not only played havoc with the fates of individual politicians enmeshed in the intrigue for power, but would ultimately alter England's capacity for self-government. Though Eliot's sympathies in any one of these given situations were never hidden, his passion for dispassionate observation resulted in a style of writing by Snow that was both analytic and introspective, one that flowed from the traditions set in motion by Jane Austen, George Eliot, and Anthony Trollope.

Unlike the other novels in the *Strangers and Brothers* series, C. P. Snow's *The Conscience of the Rich* did not involve itself with either the machinations of a group of masters at a college or the maneuverings of civil service officials in a defense ministry. Instead, it centered on the interrelationships of an enormously wealthy Anglo-Jewish merchant-banking family in their town house in Bryanston Square, London. Here Lewis Eliot was concerned not only with the destructive effects of power exercised by March *père*, Leonard, or Mr. L. as he was called, on March *fils*, Charles, but also with the wrenchings and distortions of Charles's inner personality which arose from quite another cause. For C. P. Snow's theme in *The Conscience of the Rich* was that while Charles's inherited wealth had originally limited his choice of vocation and therefore denied him freedom, his Jewishness compounded his sense of shame at being an alien, albeit a successful one, in a society that would never accept him wholly. Therefore his was a "sick conscience."

Briefly, while the plot of the novel read like a good scenario, it also served as a frame for Charles's psychological complexities and pinpoints his father's authoritarian eccentricities. At the very outset of the novel, Charles, a classmate of Eliot's, refused, after he had handled himself well in his first case in court, to continue with his chosen profession. He would not remain a lawyer because he feared that this was the course that all bright, rich young Jews of his class and community were destined to take. Instead, he chose medicine and married the daughter of a doctor; his wife was Jewish and a contributor to a Communist journal. He incurred the wrath of his father and the opposition of his assorted relatives for his break with tradition. Charles's fight for independence appeared to be more damaging to his father's ego than was his sister Katherine's marriage to Francis Getliffe, a young Cambridge physicist who was a Christian. Eliot observed that by marrying a Jewess "in the orthodox manner," Charles rationalized his defection from the legal profession and compensated for his sister's alliance with a Gentile. But Eliot was not certain that Charles's marriage would free him from self-doubts. The remainder of the novel's plot then fulfilled Eliot's pessimistic appraisal. A rejected lover of Charles's radical wife managed to create a government crisis by implicating Charles's uncle, Sir Philip, a Cabinet minister, in unethical behavior, while Charles's wife, to uphold her Marxist beliefs, refused to release certain materials that would have lifted the shadow of suspicion from the March establishment. At the very end, Charles's father cut him off completely from his inheritance.

The patent objective of this novel was to show the decline in power of a wealthy Jewish banking house, modeled closely on that of the Rothschilds. But some of the attitudes it presented vis-à-vis twentieth-century British Jews might have been as commonly prevalent as those held by Mr. Gilman in *Loyalties*, who had come forward to bolster Dancy's reputation. Though the Marches were all sober, clever people "who had got on so," Katherine March had balked at going to socials composed exclusively of Jewish young people, while Charles himself was ashamed of his heritage. Snow would have his readers believe that Leonard March was more distressed at his son's marrying a girl of his own faith, but of leftist leanings, than at his daughter Katherine's becoming the wife of a Gentile academician. The connection between Jews and wealth had by now acquired a new aspect.

To this composite portrait of the wealthy Jewish merchant and the rebellious son, Snow had on another occasion added a scientific genius who was a Jew by accident of birth. David Rubin in *Corridors of Power* was really no different from his Christian counterpart, Francis Getliffe, in *The Conscience of the Rich*. Yet of David Rubin, Snow has written

> He was the most polite of men. He had been born in Brooklyn, his parents still spoke English as a foreign language. But he had his own kind of assurance, it did not surprise him to be told that he was the favorite for that year's Nobel physics prize.[34]

Could the ascription of assurance to David Rubin in spite of his alien origin have been anything but another example of stereotypical thinking? Again, when Eliot introduced Francis Getliffe's daughter, Penelope, who was in love with a wealthy young scion of impeccable Anglo-Saxon lineage, the reader was told:

Alienation and the Cult of the Individual

> She was nineteen . . . Junoesque and in a rosy, flowering fashion, beautiful . . . Where that particular style of beauty came from, no one could explain; if I had not known, it would not have occurred to me that her mother was Jewish.[35]

Despite his analytical tendencies, the author could not help but think of Jews in preconceived and standardized terms.

Once such type casting led him to affirm that Jews were superior intellectually to non-Jews. This observation was not in keeping with the impartial tone Snow usually consigned to Lewis Eliot in the *Strangers and Brothers* series.[36]

One of the constant factors in an analysis of anti-Semitic attitudes would be attributing superior intelligence to Jews, an intelligence frequently associated with a certain unscrupulousness of character. If on the other hand Gentiles somehow were lacking in certain Christian mental endowments, they more than compensated for it by virtuous traits of temperament and personality. In several essays and articles, George Orwell, an earlier contemporary of Snow's, showed his awareness of such judgments; he regarded them as part of that larger irrationality which he equated with anti-Semitism in Britain during the two or more decades before the Second World War. But he was, at best, only able to describe its manifestations. Jews, he presumed, competed with native Britons for employment and housing; during the war years they profited from goods and services that arose in connection with the black market; had Hitler not persecuted them, they would have applauded his policies and economics; as German refugees they frequently denigrated British taste, customs, and manners. And on one occasion Orwell himself apparently believed that, at the height of the Blitz, Jews availed themselves in larger numbers than any other group of the shelters in the London Tube. On the other hand, the author refused to accept the canard that Jews were responsible for the deaths of one hundred citizens; when a bomb bursting nearby caused them to flee to the entrance of an underground station, the victims died in the crush. Still, the basic question as to why the Jews should have served as the scapegoat during the trying days of World War II eluded Orwell. While he would have urged the application of scientific methods to determine the root causes of anti-Semitism, he realized that this was not feasible. Many Britishers who might have had innate feelings of anti-Semitism would never own up to them at a time when Jews were being destroyed by Hitler. For this reason Orwell imagined that the English sense of decency would have revolted at more overt manifestations of anti-Semitism. This also made for an effective censorship of more forthright expressions of prejudice in a majority of the newspapers. What passed for anti-Semitic statements were then to be found in the everyday conversations and remarks of ordinary citizens, in the writings of the pro-Fascist groups, of the intelligentsia, and of the pacifists.[37]

If we judge his essays, Orwell's own view of anti-Semitism was that of the rational, liberal intellectual, opposed to tyranny at all costs. He regarded anti-Semitism as a popular neurosis incapable of eradication, an element that had always existed in Britain and that spread ultimately from the lower to the middle classes. However, such factors as the traditional British respect for law and the rights of the individual, the relative security of the country in the decades preceding the Second World War, and the very civilized tone of British society inhibited any truly radical growth of anti-Semitism.[38]

Orwell was noted more for his influence as an essayist and journalist than for his effects on others as a writer of fiction. His treatment of the imagined Jew in that well-known negative utopia *1984*, written shortly before his death, however, would give the lie to his reasoned thinking elsewhere, that the gentleness of the British way of life would militate against an extreme outburst of hatred against the Jew. In the nightmare world of *1984*, society was divided into three superstates, each one always in conflict with the other two on the periphery of empire. Here, the Jew had already acquired the dubious distinction of being public enemy number one, in the superstate that mattered in the novel, *Oceania*. It was highly probable that in *1984*, the Jew himself, Emanuel Goldstein, as the arch villain of the piece, did not even exist as a character; rather, he was the corporate imaginative creation of the leaders of the state. As an oligarchy that formed the *Inner Party*, these leaders had to fashion an object upon whom all human energies, formerly directed into avenues of sex, ambition, and power, could now be unleashed. That object then became the Jew, and man's normal drives, originally committed to love, to the need for interpersonal relationships, and to a sense of achievement for work well done, were now all transformed to hate. The weekly two-minute hate sessions aimed at televised pictures of Emanuel Goldstein, the obscure intellectual traitor directing a conspiracy, served the vital function of energy release for all of Oceania's population—for the leaders of the Inner Party and the Outer Party, and for the Proles, or proletariat, whose only purpose was to breed others like themselves to form the mass population of the state.

Essentially, *1984* is a journalistic novel that depicted a future science-fiction horror world, where war was peace, ignorance was strength, freedom was slavery, and every word in the language was to have only one meaning. Its rather thin plot was the story of the successful obliteration of Winston Smith's human qualities by a member of the Inner Party, O'Brien, who may or may not have been the idol, Big Brother, that the populaton at large was forced to worship. Winston Smith was destroyed as a human being because he himself dared to seek historical truth. Yet the key issue in *1984* was neither Smith's search for common reality, nor the fact that he and his girl friend, when confronted with the more immediate dangers of torture, betray each other to the authorities, but that Orwell recognized the relationship between alienation and power only too well. For Orwell viewed power as truly successful only when all human ties, bonds, relationships, and emotions were destroyed. Basically, Julia and Winston Smith betrayed each other because the naked power of government to which they had always been subjected had first destroyed the sense of fellowship between any two people. Here was power used in a totally different fashion from the way it was in the worlds of Snow's novels. There, the overriding considerations were always the means by which the individual and the group in any given situation manipulated each other in the interests of power. But in *1984*, Orwell clearly established the belief that at some time in the future in Western society, power would simply be worshiped for its own sake. In one of those excruciatingly painful series of interrogations, O'Brien admitted that his own demise, or that of any other leader, was of no moment, for power, always to be adored for its own sake, would insure the eternal existence of Oceania. But such power became effective only after the very quality of warm emotional relationships among thinking people had been eradicated by members of the Inner Party. In other words, total alienation of individuals from each other, was the single element that allowed them to be ruled by others, that permitted naked power to hold sway.

And of course the third element, besides alienation and power, had to be the Jew, to serve as the object on whom all of man's energies, released and transformed into hate, could wreak their vengeance. Under the circumstances it would appear rather simplistic to be overly concerned as to whether or not Emanuel Goldstein represented Leon Trotsky in a novel considered by some to have been a vicious parody of Stalin's Russia. For Orwell's Goldstein fulfilled a far greater role than that ever allotted to Trotsky. After all, Trotsky was assassinated, but Orwell's villain had to be maintained forever, and hence could not be allowed to appear ludicrous as his medieval Jewish forebear of a devil did. Goldstein, in fact, had to remain eternally sinister, otherwise what would become of a negative Utopia if its inhabitants could not continually refresh their own sense of virtue by coming into contact with the wellsprings of palpable evil? This, then, was the image of the Jew to which utter alienation and the worship of power had led.

7
Summary

FROM Chaucer's day until the present, Christian writers have seen the Jew as an alien in the midst of English society. They have justified this view by insisting that the Jew had always related in some evil fashion to money and to the desire for power over others. Through the centuries, relationships between Jews and Christians in England changed because of different historical developments, but the image of the Jew found in Christian literature still found its rationale in his supposedly alien qualities. Every literary era from the days of the Norman invasion to the twentieth century has borne witness to this thesis. It is the one constant factor in the Christian composite portrait of the Jew in English literature.

By recounting a version of the blood-libel legend, Chaucer's *Prioress* neatly summed up the attitudes of the Medieval Church toward the Jews. Even after they had been expelled from England in 1290, Jews were still regarded as devils, usurers, Christ-killers, swindlers, liars, thieves, and cheats, outside the closed, hierarchical scheme of God's ordered universe. They were also endowed in legend with being the artificers of blood-curdling deeds.

Such themes repeated themselves with regularity in the medieval Mystery plays, which vilified Jewish characters or turned them into grotesques for the amusement of the audience. The same pejorative attitudes toward Jews as were exemplified in these works were also to be found in *The Prioresses Tale*, based on a story of one of the miracles attributed to the Virgin Mary. Whether Chaucer himself believed what he allowed his gentle Prioress to say has been questioned, but evidence has been gathered here to show that Chaucer was very much a man of his age. For him and for other medieval writers, Jews were still the "demonic aliens."

The coming of the Renaissance, with its emphasis on man's capacity to bend the resources of the universe to his will, contributed a slightly different perspective to the image of the Jew in English literature. He was still of the devil's party, and still possessed all those loathsome qualities common to moneylenders. But by now he had allegedly acquired an uncanny ability to add power to his wealth, and to use it for international purposes. The Elizabethan villain of a stage Jew was thus able to evoke bitter envy and grudging admiration from his Christian audience. This was best exemplified by Barabas in Marlowe's *Jew of Malta*, and to a lesser degree by Shylock, in *The Merchant of Venice*, whose financial successes were a constant reproach to Antonio.

Shakespeare's genius at characterization momentarily lifted Shylock above that fiendish caricature in which Barabas and other Jewish moneylenders had customarily been grounded. On occasion, Shylock's genuine human emotions seem to have added a sense of tragic grandeur to his character, a grandeur over which some later critics and actors waxed sentimental. But despite his artistic enlargement, Shylock remained an illusory character. He was not an authentic Jew, nor was Portia a real woman. The client whose case she so brilliantly argued was an unheard-of entity—a merchant who lent money gratis and refused to take interest. The play itself was likewise a fantasy, and its Jewish miser, for all of his excursions into the realm of human feeling, was as strange and alien as his medieval ancestor, the Jew devil of the Mystery plays.

Despite historic differences between the Medieval and

Renaissance periods, it would appear that writers perceived Jews in pretty much the same way throughout those years. Artistically, of course, the generalized view of the evil Jews' plotting in *The Prioresses Tale* was quite different from the specific skulduggery of Marlowe's Barabas, or from Shylock's more sophisticated villainy. But essentially, for Marlowe and Shakespeare, the Jew was still very much what medieval Christian society had conjured him up to be in Chaucer's day. The medieval heritage of *The Merchant of Venice* had consigned Shylock to the money-grubbing realities of the Rialto. Only the new people, Antonio, Portia, Bassanio, and their friends were fit inhabitants of the idealized Belmont.

Puritan comprehension of the uses of wealth molded Jewish usurers to different proportions from those of their medieval predecessors. The horror of Christian associations with such moneylenders, international or otherwise, diminished when Cromwell, relying on Calvin's view that lending at moderate rates of interest was acceptable church doctrine, paved the way for the Jews to return to England. At the same time, reinvigorated millenial hopes prompted Christian writers to refurbish those medieval alternatives of death or conversion as the ultimate affirmation of the reigning faith. Without invoking the usual dire penalties, poets and essayists from John Donne to Abraham Cowley urged the Jews to accept Christianity. Formally, the emphases were upon Christianity's Hebraic roots and on the need for Jews to acquire spiritual grace. Yet neither Milton's appeals to right reason, nor the deistic thinking of the Cambridge Platonists proved essential for the Jews to take up quarters in England once again. More to the point was the conviction of Oliver Cromwell and his associates that legitimizing Jewish residence in England would prove beneficial to the trade of the realm. Finally, in a spirit of omission rather than commission, Cromwell recognized Jews as being present in his country. Thereupon, criticism of Jewish usurers grew muted in official governmen-

Notes

Introduction

1. Hijman Michelson, *The Jew in Early English Literature* (Amsterdam, 1926; reprinted. New York: Hermon Press, 1972), p. 14; Harm Reijndert Sientjo Van Der Veen, *Jewish Characters in Eighteenth Century Fiction and Drama* (Batavia, 1935; reprint ed. New York: Ktav Publishing House, 1973), pp. 43-46, 260-63; Edgar Rosenberg, *From Shylock to Svengali: Jewish Stereotypes in English Fiction* (Stanford, Calif., 1960), part 2; Montagu Frank Modder, *The Jew in the Literature of England* (Phila.: Jewish Publication Society, 1944), pp. 157-81; Harold Fisch, *The Dual Image: A Study of the Jew in English Literature* (London: World Jewish Library, 1972).
2. Cited in Michelson, *The Jew in Early English Literature*, pp. 42, 48-49.
3. Jacob Lopes Cardozo, *The Contemporary Jew in the Elizabethan Drama* (Paris, 1925; reprint ed. N. Y.: Burt Franklin, n. d.), p. 68.
4. Modder, *The Jew in the Literature of England*, pp. 126–55; Michelson, *The Jew in Early English Literature*, pp. 53-54; Van der Veen, *Jewish Characters*, pp. 321-28; Rosenberg, *From Shylock to Svengali*, pp. 187-258.

Chapter 1

1. *Barbarian Europe, Great Ages of Man Series* (New York: Time-Life Books, n.d.), p. 147.
2. Friedrich W. Heer, *The Medieval World, 1130-1500* (New York: New American Library, 1961), pp. 55-62.
3. Cecil Roth, *A History of the Jews in England* (Oxford: Clarendon Press, 1941), pp. 5-47.
4. Edward Flannery, *The Anguish of the Jews: Twenty-three Centuries of Anti-Semitism* (New York: Macmillan, Quest Books, 1965), pp. 25, 310-12; Roth, *History of the Jews*, pp. 21-34; James Parkes, "Jewish-Christian Relations in England," in *Three Centuries of Anglo-Jewish History*, ed. V. D. Lipman (Cambridge: Wm. Heffer & Sons, 1961), p. 149;

Salo W. Baron, *A Social and Religious History of the Jews*, 2nd ed., revised and enlarged (Philadelphia & New York: Jewish Publication Society & Columbia University Press, 1960-73), 11:146-57.
5. Flannery, *Anguish*, p. 161; Roth, *History of the Jews*, pp. 39-40.
6. Heer, *Medieval World*, pp. 123-24, 177, 253, 303, 313-16.
7. Roth, *History of the Jews*, p. 78.
8. Geoffrey Chaucer, *The Poetical Works of Chaucer*, ed. Frank N. Robinson (Cambridge, Mass.: Houghton Mifflin, 1933), p. 194.
9. Baron, *Social and Religious History*, 11: 104; Joseph Jacobs, *The Jews of Angevin England* (New York: Longmans Green, 1893), pp. xv-xvii.
10. Baron, *Social and Religious History*, 10: 97.
11. Roth, *History of the Jews*, pp. 71-90.
12. Roth, *Essays and Portraits in Anglo-Jewish History* (Philadelphia: Jewish Publication Society, 1962), pp. 2, 4-5, 42-43, 48-51.
13. Robinson, ed., *Poetical Works of Chaucer*, p. 181.
14. Ralph Baldwin, "Chronology: Space, Time in the Prologue"; Arthur W. Hoffman, "Chaucer's Prologue to Pilgrimage; The Two Voices"; John Livingston Lowes, "The Human Comedy," all in *Discussions of the Canterbury Tales*, ed. Charles A. Owen, Jr. (Boston: D. C. Heath paperback, 1961), pp. 26, 11-17, 105-9.
15. Morton W. Bloomfield, "Chaucer's Sense of History," *Discussions*, p. 104, disagrees with this view.
16. D. W. Robertson, Jr., *A Preface to Chaucer: Studies in Medieval Perspective* (Princeton, N.J.: Princeton University Press, 1968), pp. 242-43.
17. Baron, *Social and Religious History*, 10: 104; Robinson, pp. 21, 188-93.
18. Robinson, ed. *Poetical Works of Chaucer*, pp. 21. 26-27.
19. Ibid., p. 187.
20. Ibid., p. 20.
21. Robert J. Schoeck, "Chaucer's Prioress; Mercy and Tender Heart," *The Bridge: A Yearbook of Judeao-Christian Studies*, ed. John M. Oesterreicher, (New York, 1956) 2: 246-53; Edwin J. Howard, *Geoffrey Chaucer* (New York: Twayne Publishers, 1964) p. 166; Eileen Power, *Medieval English Nunneries* (Cambridge: Cambridge University Press, 1922), pp. 70, 77. 78, 80, 82.
22. Hoffman, "The Two Voices"; E. Talbot Donaldson, "Chaucer, The Pilgrim"; George L. Kittredge, "The Shipman and the Prioress"; Charles Muscatine, "The Mixed Style," all in Owen, ed., *Discussions*, pp. 14-15, 19-20, 34-36, 58.
23. Cited in Hoffman, "The Two Voices," p. 13.
24. Ibid., pp. 13-14; Kittredge, "Shipman and Prioress," pp. 34-5.
25. Baron, *Social and Religious History*, 10: 154-70.
26. Roth, *History of the Jews*, pp. 55-57; Parkes, "Jewish-Christian Relations," pp. 149-50.
27. See Robert D. French, *A Chaucer Handbook* (New York: F. S. Crofts

tal circles, while it expanded among disaffected aristocrats and middle-class merchants.

Because the Restoration and the eighteenth century were periods of wit and reason, the villainy of the Jewish usurers was rescaled for comic purposes. No longer were they incarnate villains who poisoned wells, or crucified children as a willful travesty of Christ's passion. Instead, the tradition of aristocratic satire in prose and verse, in the writings of Dryden and Pope and Swift, made effective use of the ludicrous aspects of Jewish villains. In the situation comedies and picaresque novels of the times, they also emerged as mindless misers. They had grown ridiculous, shaped by wealth into buffoons and lotharios trying to scale the social ladder. In their absurd attire and speaking some outlandish dialect, they appeared as alienated as their medieval forebears. This was now the composite picture of the average Jewish miser as he appeared in the works of middle-class poets, novelists, and dramatists, who rang all the changes upon his proverbial financial assets. For Daniel Defoe, Tobias Smollett, Henry Fielding, Samuel Richardson, and many others, the Jew had to use his wealth to maintain strumpets and frustrate the financial schemes of honest Christians. What intellectuals had complained of in this rational age—that the Jews were a necessary evil in a perfectly balanced world—popular writers were proving in their stories and dramas. And over all that dislike for the Jews there hovered an intense resentment concerning any wealth they may have accumulated. In time, the effects of such assets upon these fictional and dramatic creatures allowed them to evolve into fops and dandies. This new tradition of the effete Jewish character then found its full justification in later descriptions of aristocratic Jews, or Christian aristocrats with Jewish tendencies, securing niches in a society that rejected them.

On the other hand, occasional sentimental portraits of kindly misers were the result either of changes in the political temper of the times, or of humanitarian impulses that accompanied a rise in sentimentalism. Tobias Smollett's incredibly beneficent miser in *The Adventures of Ferdinand, Count Fathom*, may have been intended as the literary equivalent of a political change of heart, when a short-lived Naturalization Bill benefiting the Jews passed Parliament. But when the law was shortly repealed because of popular opposition to it, literary characterizations of good Jews also faded from the scene. The exception was Richard Cumberland's play, *The Jew*, depicting a miser who starved himself to aid impecunious Christians. This served as a dull offering upon the altar of English tolerance. Its sentimentalism was due in part to the incipient romanticism of the times. Sir Walter Scott's shaping of Rebecca in *Ivanhoe* was also based on those altered perceptions concerning emotion and characterization in literature. Scott's views of Rebecca may indeed have been influenced by those intricate displays of feeling with which Samuel Richardson had earlier endowed his virtuous heroine Clarissa Harlowe.

In a different context, romanticism gave new impetus to that old legend of the Wandering Jew, who, having rejected Christ, was doomed to roam the earth endlessly. His conversion and, by implication, the conversion of his race, which the medievalists had demanded upon pain of death, and for which seventeenth-century metaphysicians pleaded, now was redirected in verse by the Romantics. Wordsworth, Coleridge, Byron, and Shelley were both attracted and repelled by his strange qualities. Sometimes the Wandering Jew was also seen as a reflection of the poets' own inner selves.

In the wake of the vast industrial and technological changes that occurred during the Victorian period, the old bugaboo of the cash-nexus, that unfortunately wealth was the only element that determined human relationships, occupied the minds of some of the greatest of writers. Almost to a man they attributed this negative obsession with wealth to Jews, and thereby helped perpetuate the vision of the Jew as an alien. This was particularly true of Dickens, Thackeray, and

Trollope. Dickens's early thief, Fagin, was the prototype for all his later villains, both Jew and Gentile, who by their meretricious hankering for wealth were bent on destroying society. Thackeray, in *Vanity Fair*, had Christians pursuing wealth with as much avidity as the nouveaux riches of *Our Mutual Friend*. Trollope's venal clergyman, Mr. Emilius, of *The Eustace Diamonds*, and Augustus Melmotte, the crooked millionaire of *The Way We Live Now*, who may have had Jewish blood in their veins, based their very existence on money.

Dickens, Thackeray, and Trollope also fixed their comic genius upon that arch aristocrat of Jewish origin, Benjamin Disraeli. In his own novels he too bewailed the nefarious uses to which wealth was put by unscrupulous individuals. But lurking behind that occult fascination with riches, which absorbed so many of Diaraeli's windy protagonists, was the author's own conviction that the Sidonias of the Jewish race, and their aides-de-camp, the Adam Bessos and Henry Baronis of this world, engaged in international finance for beneficent ends. To Disraeli's detractors, however, such ubiquitous money merchants were dubious characters at best, who by their financial speculations advanced the cause of the Jewish race, but yet deceived the world. The heady rhetoric of the Prime Minister's novels, dealing with the alleged superiority of the "Arabian Race," of whom the Jews were presumably the first offspring, lent credence to Disraeli's critics. However, the Prime Minister was firmly convinced that England would be rejuvenated by the message of the eternal traditions coming form the East—from Sinai and Calvary. Implicit in his view of a reawakened England was the social and political emancipation of the Jewish community.

A more immediate result of Disraeli's aspirations was Dickens's caricature of him as James Harthouse, the dandified seducer of *Hard Times*. Disraeli's fictional creations were also the butts of Thackeray's humor—the American consul at Jerusalem, in *Notes of a Journey from Cornhill to Grand Cairo*, who reached the Holy City to await the millennium; the sultry heroine, Miriam, in *Codlingsby*, who parodied Eva of *Tancred*; and Codlingsby himself, whose diction echoed the asinine sentiments of many of Disraeli's heroes. Not to be outdone, Trollope based his characterization of Ethelbert Stanhope, the ne'er-do-well of *Barchester Towers*, on Lady Bertie, another character in *Tancred*, and modelled the "Jew-priest" of *The Eustace Diamonds* on Disraeli himself.

Such negative views of aristocrats with "Jewish" ambitions eager to transform English society, or of Jews as the proprietors of misbegotten wealth, helped perpetuate an alienated image of the Jew in literature. His distinctiveness was further intensified by the prevailing passion for racial classification. The two parameters of Darwinian philosophy were applied to distinctive groups everywhere. Were they fit to survive and had their evolution into their present state shown them to have been in lock-step agreement with progress? Even authors who might have been interested in the religious, ethnic, and cultural values of the Jewish group contributed to this overriding concern with race. George Eliot was later claimed as the prophet of a restored Zion because of her novel *Daniel Deronda*, yet she did not eschew racist qualities in her descriptions of her Jewish characters. Toward the end of the century, such perceptions about Jews sometimes degenerated into obscene physical descriptions. This is what George Du Maurier's *Trilby* was all about.

Alone of the Victorians, Robert Browning seemed free from anti-Semitic prejudice. This may have been owing to his vast erudition, to his profound insight into human personality, and perhaps to the fact he lived in Italy for many years. But his sensible comprehension of Jews and Jewish culture was not truly representative of the historical period in which he lived, and his search for a rational balance in life was not to endure. Instead, the religious, economic, and political contests which tore Victorian society apart led to the alienation of modern man. Other psychological and sociological factors reinforced this sense of individual isolation so prevalent in modern times.

In their treatment of the Jews, writers now reacted against that period by dealing with them as rootless individuals in a stream-of-consciousness technique, or by resorting to older styles of writing where many of the accepted notions as to how Jews think and believe were merely variations on earlier literary treatments. Always the rebel, Shaw delighted in reversing the theme of the Jew's association with money and with the devil. In Shaw's topsy-turvy world, millionaire bankers benefited others through man-made wars, and the devil, as Jew, guarded dull virtues in hell. Joyce's Jew, Bloom, was no longer the devil in hell, but isolated in the world. Like man himself, Joyce contended, the Jew was dispossessed. Bloom suffered both from an inability to communicate with others and from a loss of his own identity. That his condition did not change at the end of the novel was part of Joyce's commentary on modern man.

Like Joyce, Greene also dealt with individuals cut off from each other. Yet his stories were traditionally structured, and his Jews were cast in the same old mold of money-mad, vile evildoers. What was new about these antagonists was they they served to undermine Christian rogues and scoundrels, who in death assumed Christlike qualities.

There was little that was new about Evelyn Waugh's Jewish characterizations. They merely carried on the usual linking of Jews with wealth and power. This was all the more surprising in that Waugh's novels themselves were satiric, rebellious, and outrageous.

The same could not be said of Maugham's well-structured stories, where his Jews were merely extensions of older stereotypes. But Maugham's contemporary, John Galsworthy, in his play, *Loyalties*, was concerned with his hero's Jewish origins and his battle for social status in a Christian society. Delving more deeply than Galsworthy into the web of alien backgrounds, C. P. Snow pitted the alleged fascination with riches and power on the part of Jews against their religious and ethnic obligations. In *The Conscience of the Rich* and *Corridors of Power*, wealth won out. For George Orwell, the seeming villainy of the Jew served as part of a larger caricature—of a world gone mad with power. The only positive development at this time was that Galsworthy, Joyce, and Orwell had come to acknowledge the irrational nature of anti-Semitic prejudice.

Essentially then, while there were some changes in Christian attitudes to Jews in English literature as civilization itself progressed from medieval to modern times, stereotypical thinking concerning Jews still repeated itself with alarming regularity. If Marlowe's Barabas cleverly manipulated international relations by his wealth and brilliance, men in Orwell's day saw the intelligence of Jews bound up with unscrupulousness of character. If Chaucer's medieval Jewry used the blood of Christian children for religious purposes, in the secular world of the nineteenth and twentieth centuries it was calmly accepted that, out of personal greed and lust for power, the Lazaruses and Sir Marcuses encouraged the possible deaths of thousands in spurious wars. And just as the ancestors of medieval Jewry were considered representatives of the devil, so in some terrible future yet unborn, their descendants would all coalesce into some universal satanic figure to be called Emanuel Goldstein or by some other comparable nomenclature. Plus ça change . . .

Notes

Introduction

1. Hijman Michelson, *The Jew in Early English Literature* (Amsterdam, 1926; reprinted. New York: Hermon Press, 1972), p. 14; Harm Reijndert Sientjo Van Der Veen, *Jewish Characters in Eighteenth Century Fiction and Drama* (Batavia, 1935; reprint ed. New York: Ktav Publishing House, 1973), pp. 43-46, 260-63; Edgar Rosenberg, *From Shylock to Svengali: Jewish Stereotypes in English Fiction* (Stanford, Calif., 1960), part 2; Montagu Frank Modder, *The Jew in the Literature of England* (Phila.: Jewish Publication Society, 1944), pp. 157-81; Harold Fisch, *The Dual Image: A Study of the Jew in English Literature* (London: World Jewish Library, 1972).
2. Cited in Michelson, *The Jew in Early English Literature*, pp. 42, 48-49.
3. Jacob Lopes Cardozo, *The Contemporary Jew in the Elizabethan Drama* (Paris, 1925; reprint ed. N. Y.: Burt Franklin, n. d.), p. 68.
4. Modder, *The Jew in the Literature of England*, pp. 126-55; Michelson, *The Jew in Early English Literature*, pp. 53-54; Van der Veen, *Jewish Characters*, pp. 321-28; Rosenberg, *From Shylock to Svengali*, pp. 187-258.

Chapter 1

1. *Barbarian Europe, Great Ages of Man Series* (New York: Time-Life Books, n.d.), p. 147.
2. Friedrich W. Heer, *The Medieval World, 1130-1500* (New York: New American Library, 1961), pp. 55-62.
3. Cecil Roth, *A History of the Jews in England* (Oxford: Clarendon Press, 1941), pp. 5-47.
4. Edward Flannery, *The Anguish of the Jews: Twenty-three Centuries of Anti-Semitism* (New York: Macmillan, Quest Books, 1965), pp. 25, 310-12; Roth, *History of the Jews*, pp. 21-34; James Parkes, "Jewish-Christian Relations in England," in *Three Centuries of Anglo-Jewish History*, ed. V. D. Lipman (Cambridge: Wm. Heffer & Sons, 1961), p. 149;

Salo W. Baron, *A Social and Religious History of the Jews*, 2nd ed., revised and enlarged (Philadelphia & New York: Jewish Publication Society & Columbia University Press, 1960–73), 11:146–57.
5. Flannery, *Anguish*, p. 161; Roth, *History of the Jews*, pp. 39-40.
6. Heer, *Medieval World*, pp. 123-24, 177, 253, 303, 313-16.
7. Roth, *History of the Jews*, p. 78.
8. Geoffrey Chaucer, *The Poetical Works of Chaucer*, ed. Frank N. Robinson (Cambridge, Mass.: Houghton Mifflin, 1933), p. 194.
9. Baron, *Social and Religious History,* 11: 104; Joseph Jacobs, *The Jews of Angevin England* (New York: Longmans Green, 1893), pp. xv-xvii.
10. Baron, *Social and Religious History*, 10: 97.
11. Roth, *History of the Jews*, pp. 71-90.
12. Roth, *Essays and Portraits in Anglo-Jewish History* (Philadelphia: Jewish Publication Society, 1962), pp. 2, 4-5, 42-43, 48-51.
13. Robinson, ed., *Poetical Works of Chaucer*, p. 181.
14. Ralph Baldwin, "Chronology: Space, Time in the Prologue"; Arthur W. Hoffman, "Chaucer's Prologue to Pilgrimage; The Two Voices"; John Livingston Lowes, "The Human Comedy," all in *Discussions of the Canterbury Tales*, ed. Charles A. Owen, Jr. (Boston: D. C. Heath paperback, 1961), pp. 26, 11-17, 105-9.
15. Morton W. Bloomfield, "Chaucer's Sense of History," *Discussions*, p. 104, disagrees with this view.
16. D. W. Robertson, Jr., *A Preface to Chaucer: Studies in Medieval Perspective* (Princeton, N.J.: Princeton University Press, 1968), pp. 242-43.
17. Baron, *Social and Religious History*, 10: 104; Robinson, pp. 21, 188-93.
18. Robinson, ed. *Poetical Works of Chaucer*, pp. 21. 26-27.
19. Ibid., p. 187.
20. Ibid., p. 20.
21. Robert J. Schoeck, "Chaucer's Prioress; Mercy and Tender Heart," *The Bridge: A Yearbook of Judeao-Christian Studies*, ed. John M. Oesterreicher, (New York, 1956) 2: 246-53; Edwin J. Howard, *Geoffrey Chaucer* (New York: Twayne Publishers, 1964) p. 166; Eileen Power, *Medieval English Nunneries* (Cambridge: Cambridge University Press, 1922), pp. 70, 77. 78, 80, 82.
22. Hoffman, "The Two Voices"; E. Talbot Donaldson, "Chaucer, The Pilgrim"; George L. Kittredge, "The Shipman and the Prioress"; Charles Muscatine, "The Mixed Style," all in Owen, ed., *Discussions*, pp. 14-15, 19-20, 34-36, 58.
23. Cited in Hoffman, "The Two Voices," p. 13.
24. Ibid., pp. 13-14; Kittredge, "Shipman and Prioress," pp. 34-5.
25. Baron, *Social and Religious History*, 10: 154-70.
26. Roth, *History of the Jews*, pp. 55-57; Parkes, "Jewish-Christian Relations," pp. 149-50.
27. See Robert D. French, *A Chaucer Handbook* (New York: F. S. Crofts

& Co., 1947, pp. 232-42; Robinson, ed. *Poetical Works of Chaucer*, pp. 194-98, 839-40.
28. Roth, *History of the Jews*, pp. 78-80; see also Flannery, *Anguish*, p. 121.
29. Albert B. Friedman ed., *The Viking Book of Ballads* (New York: Viking, 1961), p. 2.
30. Hoffman, "The Two Voices," p. 14; Donaldson, "Chaucer", pp. 19-20, 24; Kittredge, "Shipman and Prioress," pp. 34-36; Bertrand Bronson, "Chaucer's Audience," *Discussions*, pp. 95-96; Muscatine, "Mixed Style," p. 58.
31. Schoeck, "Chaucer's Prioress", p. 253.
32. Baron, *Social and Religious History*, II: 146-48; Schoeck, "Chaucer's Prioress," pp. 255-56.
33. Baron, *Social and Religious History*, 10: 105-15; Flannery, *Anguish*, pp. 89-95; Roth, *History of the Jews*, pp. 56-88.
34. See n. 27.
35. Baron, *Social and Religious History,* 10: 148-50; Parkes, "Jewish-Christian Relations," pp. 125-26.
36. Baron, *Social and Religious History,* 11: 156-57, 175-76.

Chapter 2

1. Cecil Roth, *A History of the Jews in England* (Oxford: Clarendon Press, 1941), pp. 135-44.
2. Jacob Lopes Cardozo, *The Contemporary Jew in the Elizabethan Drama* (Paris, 1925; reprint ed. (New York: Burt Franklin, n.d.,) pp. 64, 67.
3. Roth, *History of the Jews*, pp. 140® 41, 143-44; William Shakespeare, *The Merchant of Venice, Variorum Shakespeare (MV)*, ed. Horace Howard Furness (Philadelphia: J. B. Lippincott, 1888), pp. 395-98.
4. John Palmer, *Political and Comic Characters of Shakespeare* (London: Macmillan, 1962), pp. 402-3, n. 1; see also *MV* p. 398, for statement that Lopez claimed he lied "in his confession 'to save himself from racking.'"
5. Roth, *History of the Jews*, pp. 141-42. See also *MV*, pp. 396-98, for opinion of Sir Sidney Lee that the courtiers knew that Lopez was a professing Jew and that Shakespeare was personally acquainted with him.
6. Cardozo, *Jew in Elizabethan Drama*, pp. 75-79; Christopher Marlowe, *The Jew of Malta*, in *Five Plays*, ed. Havelock Ellis (New York: Hill and Wang, 1956) Mermaid Dramabook Paperback, pp. 197-266; Myer Jack Landa, *The Jew in Drama* (1926; reprint ed. New York: Ktav Publishing House, 1969), pp. 58-60.
7. *MV*, pp. 322-24.
8. Ibid., p. 321; see also pp. 297-320.

9. Marchette Chute, *Shakespeare of London* in *Four English Biographies*, eds. J. B. Priestley & O. B. Davis (New York: Harcourt Brace & World, 1961), p. 125.
10. Hermann Sinsheimer, *Shylock, The History of a Character* (New York: B. Bloom, 1968), pp. 80-81. Cf. Palmer, *Political and Comic Characters*, pp. 420-21.
11. Henry Buckley Charlton, *Shakespearean Comedy* (New York: Macmillan, 1938), pp. 139-45, 147-48, 150-51.
12. Caesar Lombardi Barber, *Shakespeare's Festive Comedy* (New York & Cleveland: World Publishing Co., Meridian Books, 1959), pp. 169-73.
13. Ibid., p. 183; *MV* 3.1 79-121; Charlton, *Shakespearean Comedy*, pp. 153–54.
14. *MV* 2.3.2-3, 17-20.
15. Arthur Mizener, ed., *Teaching Shakespeare* (New York: New American Library, Mentor Books, pp. 89-95; Ernest Redekop, *Introduction* to *The Merchant of Venice* (New York: Airmont Classics, 1965), pp. xvii-xxv; Derek A. Traversi, *An Approach to Shakespeare* (Garden City, N.Y.: Doubleday, 1969), pp. 197-99, 202-3.
16. Murray Roston, *Introduction* to Landa, *Jew in Drama*, p. xii.
17. Palmer, *Political and Comic Characters*, p. 426.
18. Mark Van Doren, *Shakespeare* (Garden City, N.Y.: Doubleday, 1953), p. 84.
19. *MV*, 5.1.74.
20. Eustace M. W. Tillyard, *The Elizabethan World Picture* (New York: Macmillan, Vantage Books, n.d.), pp. 1-60.
21. *MV*, pp. 407-8.
22. Barber, *Shakespeare's Festive Comedy*, p. 183; Palmer, *Political and Comic Characters*, p. 427.
23. See pp. 48, 57.
24. Sinsheimer, *Shylock*, pp. 125-31.

Chapter 3

1. Basil Willey, *The Seventeenth-Century Background* (London: Chatto & Windus, 1946), pp. 149, 153-69); Eustace M. W. Tillyard, *Milton* (London: Penguin & Chatto & Windus, Peregrine Books), pp. 181-89.
2. Willey, *Seventeenth-Century*, p. 115
3. Itrat Husain, *The Dogmatic and Mystical Theology of John Donne* (New York: Macmillan, 1958), p. 106; Douglas Bush, *English Literature in the Earlier Seventeenth Century* (Oxford: Clarendon Press, 1946), pp. 243-44, 304-8.
4. Bush, *English Literature*, p. 312.
5. Ibid., p. 248; see also Tillyard, *Milton*, pp. 195-96, 230-31, but see pp.

236-44 for Milton's departure from orthodox Christian belief as demonstrated in the "unconscious meaning" of *Paradise Lost*.

6. Thomas Browne, *Religio Medici* in Boethius, *The Consolation of Philosophy*, intro., Irwin Edman (New York: Random House, Inc., 1943), pp. 330, 348.

7. Cited in Harold Fisch, *The Dual Image: A Study of the Jew in English Literature* (London: World Jewish Library, 1972), pp. 40-41; Edwin Honig an Oscar Williams, eds., *Major Metaphysical Poets of the Seventeenth Century* (New York: Simon and Schuster, 1969), p. 452; Herbert C. Grierson and Geoffrey Bullough, eds., *Oxford Book of Seventeenth Century Verse* (1934; reprint ed., London: Oxford University Press, 1966), p. 783.

8. Willey, *Seventeenth-Century*, p. 228.

9. Tillyard, Milton, pp. 183-98; Marjorie H. Nicolson, *Milton: A Reader's Guide to His Poetry* (New York: Farrar, Straus and Giroux, Noonday Press, 1963), pp. 183-241; Willey, *Seventeenth-Century*, p. 255; Harris F. Fletcher, *Milton's Semitic Studies and Some Manifestations of Them in His Poetry* (1926; reprint ed. New York: Gordian Press, 1966), pp. 129-37.

10. John Milton, *Animadversions....in The Prose Works of John Milton*, introd. Rufus Wilmot Griswold (Philadelphia: J. W. Moore, 1853) 1:107.

11. John Milton, *Of Reformation...in England*, in *Works*, supra, 1:33-34.

12. John Milton, *From the Second Defence.....*, in *Works*, trans. Robert Fellows, supra, 2:521.

13. Bush, *English Literature*, p. 156.

14. Maurice Ashley, *England in the Seventeenth Century, The Pelican History of England*: 6, 3rd ed. rev. (1961; reprint, London: Penguin Books, 1968), p. 112.

15. Cecil Roth, *A History of the Jews in England* (Oxford: Clarendon Press, 1941), p. 157.

16. Ibid., pp. 159-66; idem, "The Mystery of the Resettlement," in *Essays and Portraits in Anglo-Jewish History* (Philadelphia; Jewish Publication Society, 1962), pp. 96-105; idem, "The Resettlement of the Jews in England in 1656," in *Three Centuries of Anglo-Jewish History*, ed. V.D. Lipman (Cambridge: Wm. Heffer & Sons), pp. 1-18.

17. Roth, *History of the Jews*, p. 169.

18. *Diary of Samuel Pepys* (reprint ed. London: Dent, 1970), 1: 441 (Oct. 14, 1663).

19. Ibid., 2: 224 (Feb. 19, 1666).

20. Roth, *History of the Jews*, pp. 179-87.

21. I take no issue with those esteemed scholars (James Parkes, Cecil Roth, and others), who detail the substantial increases in legal and political rights extended to the Jews by Parliament in the eighteenth, and more particularly, in the nineteenth centuries. However, one should not confuse intolerance with alienation. Though intolerance as official policy all but disappeared in twentieth-century England, alienation persisted.

Chapter 4

1. Joseph Addison, *Sir Roger de Coverley Papers* (Cambridge, Mass: Houghton Mifflin, 1928), p. 3.
2. Cecil Roth, *A History of the Jews in England* (Oxford: Clarendon Press, 1941), pp. 191-95; Montagu Frank Modder, *The Jew in the Literature of England* (Philadelphia: Jewish Publication Society, 1944), pp. 46-48.
3. James Picciotto, *Sketches of Anglo-Jewish History*, rev. ed., Israel Finestine (London: Soncino Press, 1956), pp. 55-59.
4. Salo W. Baron, *A Social and Religious History of the Jews* (New York: Columbia University Press, 1927), 2:180.
5. Ibid., 2:180-87; ibid., 2nd ed. rev. & enl. (New York & Philadelphia: Columbia University Press and Jewish Publication Society, 1967), 13:295.
6. Cecil Roth, *Essays and Portraits in Anglo-Jewish History* (Philadelphia: Jewish Publication Society, 1962), pp. 3-4.
7. William Shakespeare, *MV*, Variorum ed. Horace Howard Furness (Philadelphia: J. B. Lippincott, 1888), Appendix, pp. 351, 355; Harm Reijndert Sientjo Ven Der Veen, *Jewish Characters in Eighteenth Century Fiction and Drama* (Batavia; 1935; reprint ed., New York: Ktav Publishing House, 1973), pp. 81-105, 165-66; Edgar Rosenberg, *Tabloid Jews and Fungus Scribblers* (1972), in Van Der Veen, *Jewish Characters*, pp. 53-54.
8. Van der Veen, *Jewish Characters*, pp. 107-41.
9. Myer Jack Landa, *The Jew in Drama* (1926; reprint ed. New York: Ktav Publishing House, 1969), pp. 133-38; Van der Veen, *Jewish Characters*, pp. 230-33.
10. Van der Veen, *Jewish Characters*, pp. 235-36.
11. *The Examiner*, April 12, 1711; also cited in Modder, *Jew in Literature*, p. 54; Van der Veen, *Jewish Characters*, p. 25.
12. Modder, *Jew in Literature*, p. 52; Van der Veen, *Jewish Characters*, pp. 29-30.
13. See Kathleen Williams, *Jonathan Swift*, Profiles in Literature Series (London: Routledge Kegan Paul, 1968), pp. 91-92, 94 for examples of Swift's scathing satire.
14. George Sherburn, ed., *The Best of Pope* (New York: Ronald Press, 1929), pp. 114-54, 406-16.
15. Van der Veen, *Jewish Characters*, p. 23.
16. Max Weber, *The Protestant Ethic and the Spirit of Capitalism* (New York: New American Library, Mentor Books, 1958), pp. 180, 270 n. 58.
17. Daniel Defoe, *Roxana Or The Fortunate Mistress*, ed. Jane Jack (London: Oxford University Press, 1964), pp. 112-29, 133-35, 139-40.
18. Daniel Defoe, *Robinson Crusoe*, (New York: New American Library, Mentor Books, 1968), pp. 213-16.
19. Tobias Smollett, *The Expedition of Humphrey Clinker* (New York: Modern Library, 1929), pp. 26-27.

20. Tobias Smollett, *The Adventures of Roderick Random*, 2 vols. in *The Works of Tobias Smollett*, 12 vols. (New York: Jensen Society, 1902), 1:94.
21. Tobias Smollett, *Peregrine Pickle* (London: J. M. Dent & Sons, Ltd., 1967), 1:273, 274-76.
22. Tobias Smollett, *The Adventures of Ferdinand, Count Fathom*, ed. Damian Grant (London: Oxford University Press, 1971), p. 228.
23. Van Der Veen, *Jewish Characters*, pp. 43-45.
24. Ibid., pp. 48-49.
25. Cited in Edgar Rosenberg, *From Shylock to Svengali, Jewish Stereotypes in English Fiction* (Stanford, Calif: Stanford University Press, 1060), p. 353 n. 30.
26. Joseph Jacobs, "The Original of Scott's Rebecca," *Publication of the American Jewish Historical Society* 23 (1914): 53-60.
27. Rosenberg, *From Shylock to Svengali*, pp. 187-205.
28. The classic formulation of the Wandering Jew legend has been stated by Modder and elaborated upon by Van der Veen and Rosenberg. The brief account here is intended merely to note that the Romantics' version of the legend, for all of the rebellious admiration it evoked, still associated Jews with money. When, however, that legend became the source for nineteenth-century Jewish wanderers, these Jews occupied themselves primarily with occult matters. Such wealth as they possessed served to highlight the problems that excessive riches would entail, but did not obscure the basic thrust of the wanderer's concern—the power that knowledge of the secret life conferred.

Chapter 5

1. Edgar Johnson, *Charles Dickens: His Tragedy and Triumph* (New York: Simon & Schuster, 1958), 2: 799; Boris Ford, ed., *Pelican Guide to English Literature, From Dickens to Hardy* (London: Pelican, 1958), 6: 1-56.
2. Steven Marcus, *Dickens from Pickwick to Dombey* (New York: Simon & Schuster, 1965), pp. 54-91.
3. Charles Dickens, *Oliver Twist* (New York: Lancer Books, 1968), p. 236.
4. Charles Dickens, *The Old Curiosity Shop* (Harmondsworth: Penguin, 1972), p. 566.
5. Charles Dickens, *Oliver Twist,* pp. 227, 242.
6. Ibid., p. 657.
7. *Old Curiosity Shop*, p. 65; Charles Dickens, *Oliver Twist*, p. 551.
8. Charles Dickens, *Old Curiosity Shop*, p. 73.
9. Walter Allen, *The English Novel: A Short Critical History* (Harmonsworth: Penguin, 1958), pp. 171-72; Marcus, *Dickens*, pp. 338® 40.

10. Charles Dickens, *Dombey and Son* (New York: Dodd Mead, 1960), p. 791.
11. Charles Dickens, *Hard Times* (London: J. M. Dent & Sons, 1960), p. 37.
12. Charles Dickens, *Our Mutual Friend* (New York: Dodd Mead, 1961), pp. 268-69.
13. Johnson, *Charles Dickens*, 2: 1010-12; *idem*, "Dickens, Fagin, and Mr. Riah," *Commentary* 9:1 (January 1950): 47-50.
14. Lionel Trilling, ed., *The Portable Matthew Arnold* (New York: Viking Press, 1949), pp. 480-82.
15. *Hard Times*, pp. 111-12.
16. Charles Dickens, *Our Mutual Friend*, pp. 441, 447, 448.
17. Charles Dickens, *Bleak House* (New York: New American Library, a Signet Classic, 1964), ppp. 174-75.
18. Benjamin Disraeli, *Coningsby* (London: Everyman Library, 1971), pp. 175-83, 207-11; *idem*, *Tancred* (London: Longmans Green, 1877), pp. 125-26, 228-29, 388-90, 398-99, 427-28.
19. Disraeli, *Tancred*, p. 196.
20. Disraeli, *Coningsby*, pp. 206-7; *idem*, *Tancred*, pp. 194-95, 265-66; *idem*, *Alroy* (London: Longmans Green, n.d.), pp. 153-56.
21. William Makepeace Thackeray, *Sketchbooks* (New York: Harper Bros., 1903), pp. 655-56, 689-90.
22. *Contributions to "Punch." The Works of William Makepeace Thackeray* (New York: Harper Bros., 1903), 6: 485-86.
23. Anthony Trollope, *Barchester Towers* (London: Oxford University Press, 1971), p. 72.
24. Anthony Trollope, *The Eustace Diamonds* (London: Oxford University Press, 1973), pp. 666, 724.
25. Cited in Walter Allen, *George Eliot* (New York: Macmillan, 1964), p. 165.
26. George Eliot, *Daniel Deronda* (Boston: D. Lathrop & Co., 1885), bk. 6, p. 125.
27. Allen, *Eliot*, pp. 169-70; Frank Raymond Leavis, *The Great Tradition: A Study of the English Novel* (New York: Doubleday, Anchor Books, 1968), pp. 101-8, 118-23, 125-38, 142-50; Basil Willey, *Nineteenth Century Studies: Coleridge to Matthew Arnold* (Harmondsworth: Penguin, Peregrine Book 1964), p. 71; Joan Bennett, "Vision and Design," in *Discussions of George Eliot*, ed. R. Stang, (Cambridge, Mass.: 1960), D. C. Heath (paperback), pp. 65-66.
28. Anthony Trollope, *The Way We Live Now* (London: Panther Books, 1969), p. 135.
29. Eliot, *Deronda*, bk. 4, p. 399; Trollope, *Eustace Diamonds*, pp. 715, 718.
30. George du Maurier, *Trilby* (London: J. M. Dent & Sons, Everyman (paperback), 1969), pp. 44-50, 83, 105, 247-50, 291-300. See Rosenberg,

From Shylock to Svengali, pp. 244-47, for du Maurier's use of the Wandering Jew image.

31. Montagu Frank Modder, *The Jew in the Literature of England* (Philadelphia: Jewish Publication Society, 1944), pp. 294-346.

32. Robert Browning, *The Poetical Works of Robert Browning*, ed. G. Robert Stange (Cambridge, Mass.: Houghton Mifflin, 1974), pp. 23, 167-68, 252, 281-82, 372, 383-85, 531, 532, 534, 549, 550, 823-27; *Jewish Encyclopedia*, 1940, 2: 364; Vernon C. Harrington, *Browning Studies* (Boston: R. C. Badger, 1915), pp. 215-68, 301-74.

Chapter 6

1. George Bernard Shaw, *Everybody's Political What's What* (New York: Doubleday, 1944), p. 287; see also Lawrence Langner, *G. B. S. and the Lunatic* (New York: Atheneum, 1963), p. 162-73, for the belief that as a nonogenarian, Shaw justified Hitler's estimate of the Jews; Eric Bentley, "The Making of a Dramatist, 1892-1903," in *George Bernard Shaw: Twentieth Century Views* (Englewood Cliffs, N.J.: Prentice-Hall, 1965), p. 58, elaborates upon Shaw's view of the nature of dramatic art.
2. S. L. Goldberg, *The Classical Temper* (London: Chatto & Windus, 1969), p. 285 n. 17.
3. James Joyce, *Ulysses* (New York: Random House, 1932), p. 324.
4. Ibid., p. 325.
5. Ibid., p. 327
6. Ibid., p. 336.
7. Ibid., p. 338-39.
8. Ibid., p. 385.
9. Ibid., pp. 387-88.
10. Ibid., pp. 400–401.
11. Ibid., pp. 402-3.
12. Ibid., pp. 454-55.
13. Ibid., pp. 477, 485-88.
14. Goldberg, *Classical Temper*, pp. 185-87, 274-75.
15. Joyce, *Ulysses*, p. 666.
16. Cf. Edmund Wilson, *Axel's Castle* (New York: Scribner's, 1959), p. 202; Goldberg, *Classical Temper*, pp. 91-93.
17. James Joyce, *Portrait of the Artist As a Young Man* (New York: Viking Press, 1965), p. 263; William York Tindall, *A Reader's Guide to James Joyce* (London: James Hudson (paperback), 1971), pp. 222-23.
18. Arnold Kettle, *An Introduction to the English Novel* (London: Hutchinson Co. (paperback), 1972), 2: 132.
19. Goldberg, *Classical Temper*, pp. 290-91, nn. 28, 29.

20. Matthew Arnold, "Dover Beach," in *English Poets, Romantic, Victorian and Later*, ed. James Stephens, Edwin L. Beck, and Royall H. Snow (New York: American Book Co., 1934), p. 563.
21. Graham Greene, *Brighton Rock*, Compass ed. (New York: Viking, 1956), p. 348.
22. Graham Greene, *This Gun for Hire* in *Three* (New York: Viking, 1952), p. 145.
23. Ibid., p. 76.
24. Ibid., pp. 146-47.
25. A. A. DeVitis, *Graham Greene*, Twayne English Authors Series 3 (New York: Twayne, 1963), p. 152.
26. Greene, *Brighton Rock*, p. 332.
27. Ibid., p. 89.
28. Ibid., p. 180.
29. Ibid., p. 257.
30. DeVitis, *Graham Greene*, pp. 147-50.
31. John Galsworthy, *Loyalties, Laurel British Drama: The Nineteenth Century*, ed. R. W. Corrigan (New York: Dell Publishing Co. [paperback], 1969), p. 191.
32. Ibid., p. 174.
33. Jerome Thale, *C. P. Snow, Writers and Critics*, (Edinburgh & London: Oliver Boyd [paperback], 1964), pp. 30, 53-54, 57.
34. C. P. Snow, *Corridors of Power* (New York: Bantam, 1965), pp. 9-10.
35. Ibid., p. 125.
36. "Why Are Jews Successful?" *Christianity Today*, 13:15, April 25, 1969, p. 31.
37. George Orwell, *As I Please*, 1943-45 in *Collected Essays, Journalism and Letters of George Orwell* (= *Collected Essays*), ed. Sonia Orwell and Ian Angus (London: Penguin, 1968), 3:332, 333, 424.
38. George Orwell, *My Country Right or Left*, in *Collected Essays* ed. Orwell and Angus, 2:229, 213, 332-33, 427-28; 3:103, 112-14, 378-88, 412, 416, 419-20, 424, 426, 430; idem, *In Front of Your Nose*, 4:227, 357.

Bibliography

Allen, Walter. *The English Novel: A Short Critical History.* Harmondsworth, England: Penguin, Pelican Books, 1958.

―――. *George Eliot.* Master of World Literature Series. New York: Macmillan, 1964.

―――. *Tradition and Dream: A Critical Survey of British and American Fiction From the 1920's to the Present Day.* Harmondsworth, England: Penguin, Pelican Books, 1965.

Arnold, Matthew. "Sweetness and Light." *The Portable Matthew Arnold.* New York: Viking Press, 1949.

Ashley, Maurice. *England in the Seventeenth Century. The Pelican History of England*:6. 1967 ed. London: Penguin, Pelican Books. 1968.

Bacon, Francis. *Essays and New Atlantis.* New York: Walter S. Black, 1942.

Barber, Caesar Lombardi. *Shakespeare's Festive Comedies.* New York & Cleveland: World Publishing Co., Meridian Books, 1959.

Baron, Salo W. *A Social and Religious History of the Jews.* 3 vols. New York: Columbia University Press, 1937.

―――. *A Social and Religious History of the Jews.* 2nd ed. rev. & enl. 15 vols. New York & Philadelphia: Columbia University Press, and Jewish Publication Society, 1960-1973.

Beck, E. L.; Snow, R. H.: et al. eds. *English Poets, Romantic Victorian and Later.* New York: American Book Co., 1934.

Blanshard, Rufus A., ed. *Discussions of Alexander Pope*. Boston: D. C. Heath (paperback), 1960.

Booth, Bradford A. *Anthony Trollope, Aspects of His Life and Art*. Bloomington: University of Indiana Press, 1958.

Bowden, Muriel. *A Reader's Guide to Chaucer*. New York: Farrar, Shaus and Giroux, Noonday Press.

Browne, Sir Thomas. *Religio Medici. The Consolation of Philosophy*. Modern Library Series. Introduction by Irwin Edman. New York: Random House, 1943.

Browning, Robert. *The Complete Poetical Works of Robert Browning*. Cambridge Edition. Cambridge, Mass.: Houghton Mifflin, 1974.

Bush, Douglas. *English Literature in the Earlier Seventeenth Century*. Oxford: Clarendon Press, 1946.

Cardozo, Jacob Lopes. *The Contemporary Jew in the Elizabethan Drama*. Essays in Literature and Criticism #5 (1925). Reprint. Burt Franklin: Research and Source Work Series #115. New York: Burt Franklin, n.d.

Charlton, Henry B. *Shakespearian Comedy*. New York: Barnes & Noble, 1938.

Chaucer, Geoffrey. *The Poetical Works of Geoffrey Chaucer*. Edited by F. N. Robinson. Cambridge, Mass.: Houghton Mifflin, 1933.

Chesterton, G. K. *Charles Dickens*. Introduction by Steven Marcus. New York: Schocken Books (paperback), 1965.

Chute, Marchette. *Geoffrey Chaucer of England*. New York: Dutton, 1946.

———. *Shakespeare of London. Four English Biographies*. Davis, O. B. and Priestley, J. B., eds. New York: Harcourt, Brace & World, 1961.

Complete Poems of Keats and Shelley. New York: Modern Library, 1931.

The Complete Poetry And Selected Prose of John Donne & The Complete Poetry of William Blake. Edited by J. Hayward and G. Keynes. New York: Random House, 1941.

Congreve, William. *The Way of the World, Restoration Plays*. New York: Modern Library, 1953.

Crump, G. M., ed. *Twentieth Century Interpretations of Samson Agonistes*. Englewood Cliffs, N. J.: Prentice Hall, 1968.

Defoe, Daniel. *Moll Flanders*. New York: New American Library, 1964.

———. *Robinson Crusoe*. New York: New American Library, 1961.

———. *Roxana; Or, The Fortunate Mistress*. Edited by Jane Jack. London: Oxford University Press, 1964.

DeVitis, A. A. *Graham Greene*. Twayne English Authors Series. Edited by S. L. Bowman. New York: Twayne Publishers, 1963.

Deutsch, Babette. *The Reader's Shakespeare*. New York: Julian Messner, 1959.

Dickens, Charles. *Bleak House*. New York: New American Library, *Signet Classic*, 1964.

———. *Dombey and Son*. New York: Dodd Mead, 1950.

———. *Great Expectations*. New York: Washington Square Press (paperback), 1963.

———. *Hard Times*. London: J. M. Dent, 1960.

———. *The Life and Adventures of Martin Chuzzlewit*. Harmondsworth, England: Penguin Books, 1972.

———. *Nicholas Nickleby*. New York: Dodd Mead, 1944.

———. *The Old Curiosity Shop*. Harmondsworth, England: Penguin Books, 1972.

———. *Oliver Twist*. New York: Lancer Books, Easy-Eye Magnum, 1968.

———. *Our Mutual Friend*. New York: Dodd Mead, 1951.

The Diary of Samuel Pepys. 1971. Reprint ed. 3 vols. London: J. M. Dent, 1973.

Disraeli, Benjamin. *Alroy*. London: Longmans Green, n.d.

———. *Coningsby*. London: Dent, 1971.

———. *Endymion*. New York: Harvard Publishing, n.d.

———. *Tancred*. London: Longmans Green, 1877.

Du Maurier, George. *Trilby*. Reprint. London: J. M. Dent, Everyman (paperback), 1969.

Edwards, Peter D. *Anthony Trollope: Profiles in Literature Series*. Edited by B. C. Southam. London: Routledge, Kegan Paul, 1968.

Eliot, George. *Daniel Deronda*. Boston: D. Lathrop & Co., 1885.

Ellis, Frank H., ed. *Twentieth Century Interpretations of Robinson Crusoe*. Englewood Cliffs, N.J.: Prentice Hall, 1969.

Fido, Martin. *Charles Dickens: Profiles in Literature Series*. Edited by B. C. Southam. New York: Humanities Press, 1968.

Fisch, Harold. *The Dual Image*. London: World Jewish Library, 1971.

Flannery, Edward H. *The Anguish of the Jews: Twenty-three Centuries of Anti-Semitism*. New York: Macmillan, Quest Books, 1965.

Ford, Boris, ed. *Pelican Guide to English Literature*. 7 vols. Harmondsworth, England: Penguin, 1954-1961.

French, Robert D. *A Chaucer Handbook*. New York: F. S. Crofts, 1947.

Friedman, Albert, ed. *The Viking Book of Folk Ballads*. New York: Viking, 1961.

Galsworthy, John. *Loyalties, Laurel British Drama*. Edited by R. W. Corrigan. New York: Dell Publishing (paperback), 1969.

Gettman, Royal Alfred, ed. *The Rime of the Ancient Mariner: A Handbook*. San Francisco: Wadsworth Publishing Co., 1961.

Goldberg, S. L. *The Classical Temper: A Study of James Joyce's Ulysses*. London: Chatto & Windus, 1969.

Granville-Barker, H. *The Merchant of Venice, Shakespeare: Modern Essays in Criticism*. Rev. ed. Edited by L. F. Dean. New York: Oxford University Press, 1967.

Greene, Graham. *Brighton Rock*. Compass Edition. New York: Viking, 1956.

―――. *This Gun for Hire*. New York: Viking, 1952.

Grierson, Hubert C., and G. Bullough, eds. *The Oxford Book of Seventeenth Century Verse*. 1934 Reprint. London: Oxford University Press, 1966.

Bibliography 185

Hanford, James Holly. *A Milton Handbook*. New York: Appleton-Century-Crofts, 1954.

Harrington, Vernon C. *Browning Studies*. Boston: R. G. Badger, 1915.

Heer, F. *The Medieval World*. New York: New American Library, 1961.

Honig, Edwin and Oscar Williams, eds. *Major Metaphyscal Poets of the Seventeenth Century*. New York: Simon & Schuster, 1969.

House, Humphrey. *The Dickens World*. London & New York: Oxford University Press, 1941.

Howard, Edwin J. *Geoffrey Chaucer*. Twayne English Authors Series. Edited by S. L. Bowman. New York: Twayne, 1964.

Husain, Itrat. *The Dogmatic and Mystical Theology of John Donne*. New York: Macmillan, 1958.

Jacobs, Joseph. *The Jews of Angevin England*. New York: Longmans Green, 1893.

Jarman, T. L. *A Short History of Twentieth Century England, 1868-1962*. New York: New American Library, Mentor Books, 1963.

Johnson, Edgar. *Charles Dickens: His Tragedy and Triumph*. New York: Simon & Schuster, 1954, 2 vols.

Joyce, James. *A Portrait of the Artist As a Young Man*. New York: Viking, 1964.

―――. *Ulysses*. New York: Random House, 1936.

Karl, Frederick R. *An Age of Fiction: The Nineteenth Century British Novel*. New York: Farrar, Straus and Giroux, 1964.

Kaufman, R. J., ed. *G. B. Shaw: A Collection of Critical Essays, Twentieth Century Views*. Englewood Cliffs, N.J.: Prentice Hall, 1965.

Kettle, Arnold. *An Introduction to the English Novel*. 2 vols. 2nd ed. reprint, 1967. London: Hutchinson & Co. Ltd., 1972.

Knight, G. W. *Shakespeare and Religion*. New York, Simon & Schuster, 1967.

Knoll, Robert E. *Christopher Marlowe*. Twayne English Authors Series. Edited by S. L. Bowman. New York: Twayne, 1969.

Landa, Myer Jack. *The Jew In Drama.* 1926 Reprint ed. New York: Ktva, 1969.

Langner, Lawrence. *G. B. S. and The Lunatic.* New York: Athenaeum, 1963.

Lauber, J. *Sir Walter Scott.* Twayne English Authors Series. Edited by S. L. Bowman. New York: Twayne, 1966.

Leavis, Frank Raymond. *The Great Tradition: A Study of the English Novel.* New York: Doubleday, 1968.

Lipman, V. D., ed. *Three Centuries of Anglo-Jewish History.* Cambridge: W. Heffer & Sons, 1961.

Lodge, D. *Graham Greene.* Columbia Essays on Modern Writers Series. No. 17. New York: Columbia University Press, 1966.

Marcus, Steven. *From Pickwick to Dombey.* New York: Simon & Schuster, 1965.

Martz, Louis. *Milton, Twentieth Century Views.* Englewood Cliffs, N.J.: Prentice Hall, 1966.

Marlowe, Christopher. *The Jew of Malta.* Edited by Havelock Ellis. New York: Hill & Wang. Mermaid Dramaback, 1956.

Maugham, W. Somerset. "Mr. Know-All." *Cosmopolitans.* New York: Doubleday, 1936.

———. *The Razor's Edge.* New York: Doubleday, 1944.

Maurois, Andre. *Disraeli: A Picture of the Victorian Age.* Translated by Hamish Miles. New York: Random House, 1928.

Michelson, Hijman. *The Jew in Early English Literature* (1924). Reprint. New York: Hermon Press, 1972.

Milton, John, *The Prose Works of John Milton.* 2 vols. Introduction by Rufus W. Griswold. Philadelphia: J. W. Moore, 1853.

Mizener, Arthur, ed. *Teaching Shakespeare.* New York: New American Library, Mentor Books, 1969.

Modder, Montagu Frank. *The Jew in the Literature of England.* Philadelphia: Jewish Publication Society, 1944.

Myers, A. R. *England in the Middle Ages. The Pelican History of England.* Rev. ed. Harmondsworth, England: Penguin Books, 1963.

Nicolson, Marjorie Hope. *John Milton: A Reader's Guide to His Poetry*. New York: Noonday Press, 1963.

Orwell, George. *1984*. New York: New American Library, Mentor Books, 1961.

Orwell, Sonia and Angus, I., eds. *Collected Essays, Journalism and Letters of George Orwell* (1941-45). 4 vols. Harmondsworth, England: Penguin Books, 1968.

Owen, Charles A. Jr., ed. *Discussions of the Canterbury Tales*. Boston: D. C. Heath (paperback) 1961.

Palmer, John. *Political and Comic Characters of Shakespeare*. London: Macmillan, Papermac 4, 1962.

Parkes, James. *A History of the Jewish People*. Harmondsworth, England: Penguin, 1964.

―――. "Jewish-Christian Relations in England." In *Three Centuries of Anglo-Jewish History*. Edited by V. D. Lipman. Cambridge: Wm. Heffer and Sons, 1961.

―――. *The Jewish Community in the Middle Ages*. London: Soncino, 1938.

Pearson, Hesketh. *G. B. S.: A Full-length Portrait*. New York: Harper, 1942.

Philipson, David. *The Jew in English Fiction*. Cincinnati, Ohio: R. Clarke, 1889.

Picciotto, James. *Sketches of Anglo-Jewish History*. Rev. ed. London: Soncino, 1956.

Plumb, J. H. *England in the Eighteenth Century*. Harmondsworth, England: Penguin, 1944.

Power, Eileen. *Medieval English Nunneries*. Cambridge: Cambridge University Press, 1922.

Richardson, Samuel. *Clarissa, Or The History of a Young Lady*. 4 vols. London: J. M. Dent, 1968.

―――. *The History of Sir Charles Grandison*. Edited by Jocelyn Harris, in three parts. London: Oxford University Press, 1972.

Robertson, D. W., Jr. *A Preface to Chaucer: Studies in Medieval Perspective*. Princeton, N. J.: Princeton University Press, 1962.

Rosenberg, Edgar. *From Shylock to Svengali: Jewish Stereotypes in English Fiction.* Stanford, California: Stanford University Press, 1960.

Roth, Cecil. *A History of the Jews in England.* Oxford: Clarendon Press, 1941.

Sale, Roger, ed. *Discussions of the Novel.* Boston: D. C. Heath (paperback), 1960.

Sargeaunt, John, ed. *Dryden's Poems.* London: Oxford University Press, 1925.

Schoeck, Robert J. "Chaucer's Prioress: Mercy and Tender Heart," *The Bridge: A Yearbook of Judaeo-Christan Studies.* Edited by J. M. Oesterreicher. New York: Pantheon Books, 1956, 2:246-53.

Scholes, R., ed. *Approaches to the Novel: Materials for Poetics.* San Francisco: Chandler Publishing Co., 1961.

Scott, Sir Walter. *Ivanhoe.* London: Nelson Classics, n.d.

Schutte, Wm. M., ed. *Twentieth-century Interpretations of A Portrait of the Artist As a Young Man.* Englewood Cliffs N.J.: Prentice Hall, 1968.

Schweitzer, Frederick M. *A History of the Jews Since the First Century A. D.* New York: Macmillan (paperback), 1971.

Shakespeare, William. *The Merchant of Venice.* Airmont Classics Series. New York: Airmont (paperback), 1965.

———. *The Merchant of Venice.* Variorum edition. Edited by H. H. Furness. Philadelphia: J. B. Lippincott, 1888.

———. *The Merchant of Venice.* Folger Edition. New York: Washington Square Press (paperback), 1957.

Shaw, George Bernard. *Everybody's Political What's What.* New York: Dodd Mead, 1944.

———. *Major Barbara.* Baltimore, Md.: Penguin Books, 1971.

———. *Seven Plays.* New York: Dodd Mead, 1941.

Sherburn, George. *The Best of Pope.* New York: Ronald Press, 1929.

Sinsheimer, Hermann. *Shylock, The History of a Character.* 1947. Reprint ed. New York: B. Bloom, 1968.

Smollett, Tobias. *The Adventures of Ferdinand, Count Fathom.* Edited by Damian Grant. London: Oxford University Press, 1971.

———. *The Adventures of Roderick Random.* 2 vols. New York: Jenson Society, 1902.

———. *The Expedition of Humphrey Clinker.* New York: Modern Library, 1929.

———. *Peregrine Pickle.* 2 vols. Introduction by Walter Allen. New York: Everyman's Library, 1967.

Snow, Charles P. *The Conscience of the Rich.* New York: Chas. Scribner's Sons, 1958.

———. *Corridors of Power.* New York: Bantam, 1965.

Southern, Leslie. *The Making of the Middle Ages.* London: Hutchinson, 1953.

Stang, Richard, ed. *Discussions of George Eliot.* Boston: D. C. Heath (paperback), 1960.

Stephen, Leslie. *English Literature and Society in the Eighteenth Century.* 1903 Reprint ed. London: G. Duckworth & Co., 1965.

Stevenson, Louis. *The English Novel, A Panorama.* Boston: Houghton Mifflin, 1960.

Tawney, R. H. *Religion and the Rise of Capitalism.* New York: New American Library, 1947.

Thackeray, William M. *Codlingsby. Novels by Eminent Hands. Contributions to "Punch."* Vol. 6. New York: Harper, 1903.

———. *Notes of a Journey from Cornhill to Grand Cairo. Sketchbooks.* New York: Harper, 1903.

———. *Vanity Fair.* New York: Dodd Mead, 1943.

Thale, Jerome. *C. P. Snow, Writers and Critics.* London: Oliver & Boyd (paperback), 1964.

Tillyard, Eustace M. W. *The Elizabethan World Picture.* New York: Macmillan/Vantage Books, n.d.

———. *Milton.* London: Penguin, & Chatto & Windus, 1968.

Tindall, William York. *A Reader's Guide to James Joyce.* London: James Hudson, 1971.

Traversi, Derek A. *An Approach to Shakespeare.* New York: Doubleday, 1959.

Trilling, Lionel, ed. *The Portable Matthew Arnold.* New York: Viking, 1949.

Trollope, Anthony. *The Way We Live Now.* Introduction by Herbert Van Thal. London: Panther Books (paperback), 1969.

Van Der Veen, Harm R. S. *Jewish Characters in Eighteenth-century Fiction and Drama.* Reprint ed. New York: Ktav, 1973.

Van Doren, Mark. *Shakespeare.* New York: Doubleday, 1953.

Van Ghent, Dorothy. *The English Novel: Form and Function.* New York: Holt, Rinehart & Winston, 1953.

Wall, Stephen. *Charles Dickens: A Critical Anthology.* Harmondsworth, England: Penguin, 1970.

Waugh, Evelyn. *Black Mischief.* Boston: Little, Brown and Company. 1946.

———. *Decline and Fall.* New York: Doubleday, 1929.

———. *Helena.* Boston: Little, Brown and Company, 1950.

———. *Men at Arms.* Boston: Little, Brown, and Company, 1952.

———. *Vile Bodies.* Boston: Little, Brown and Company, 1977.

Weber, Max. *The Protestant Ethic and the Spirit of Capitalism.* New York: New American Library, Mentor Books, 1958.

Welsh, Arthur, ed. *Thackeray: A Collection of Critical Essays, Twentieth Century Views.* Englewood Cliffs, N.J.: Prentice Hall, 1968.

Willey, Basil. *The Eighteenth Century Background.* London: Chatto & Windus, 1946.

———. *Nineteenth Century Studies: Coleridge to Matthew Arnold.* Harmondsworth, England: Penguin, Peregrine Books, 1974.

———. *The Seventeenth Century Background.* London: Chatto & Windus, 1946.

Williams, Kathleen. *Jonathan Swift.* Profiles in Literature Series. Edited by B. C. Sotham. London: Routledge, Kegan Paul, 1968.

Wilson, Edmund. *Axel's Castle: A Study in the Imaginative Literature of 1870-1930*. New York: Chas. Scribner's Sons, 1931.

———. *A Piece of My Mind: Reflections at Sixty*. New York: Doubleday, 1958.

Wyndham, Francis. *Graham Greene*. Writers and Their Work: No. 67. Edited by Geoffrey Bullough. London: Longmans Green, 1966.

Index

Abigail, 45
Age of Bronze (Byron), 102
American Consul at Jerusalem. *See* Warder Cresson
Amsterdam Jewish Community, 75, 81
Anglican Church, 67–68, 75, 88, 91, 110
Anne, queen of England, 81, 84
Antonio, 47–50, 52–54, 56–57, 59, 61–62, 163–64; and anti-Semitism, 48–50; attitude toward wealth, 47–49, 53–54
Arnold, Ida, 146–48
Arnold, Matthew, 112, 124, 141–42; *Dover Beach*, 141–42

Bacon, Francis, 65–66, 90
Barchester Towers (Trollope), 116
Barabas, 14–15, 44–46, 82, 84, 128, 153, 164, 170. *See also* Image of the Jew as devil; Image of the Jew as manipulator of wealth and power
Bassanio, 44, 47–48, 50–55, 59–60, 164
Belmont, 50, 52–54, 56–57, 59–61, 63, 90
Bishop Orders His Tomb at St. Praxed's Church, The (Browning), 124
Ben Israel, Rabbi Manasseh, 75–76
Bertie, Lady (*Tancred*), 116, 168
Big Brother, 159
Bleak House (Dickens), 113–14
Blood libel, 23–41, 162, 170; Chaucer's attitude toward, 28–31, 33, 38, 40. *See also* Hugh of Lincoln legend

Bloody Tenent of Persecution, The (Williams), 73
Bloom, Leopold, 16, 96, 131–41, 169
Bloom, Molly, 130–31, 137, 140–41
Bloom, Rudy, 131, 140
Bois-Guilbert, Brian de, 97–99
Bouillon, Godfrey de, Marquis of Codlingsby, 115–16
Bounderby, Josiah, 108–9
Breen, Mrs. Josephine, 130
Breghert, Ezekiel, 120
Brown, Pinkie, 142, 146–48
Brown, Rose, 146–47
Browne, Sir Thomas, 65, 68–69. *See also* Jews, conversion of
Browning, Robert, 18, 37, 124–26, 130, 168; attitude toward Jews, 124–26, 168. Works: *Bishop Orders His Tomb at St. Praxed's Church, The*, 124; *Filippo Baldinucci on the Privilege of Burial*, 125; *Holy-Cross Day*, 125; *Jochanan Hakkadosh*, 125; *My Last Duchess*, 124; *Rabbi Ben Ezra*, 125; *Ring and the Book, The*, 125; *Soliloquy of the Spanish Cloister*, 124
Byron, George Gordon, Lord, 101–2, 122; *Age of Bronze*, 102

Cain, 101
Calvinism, 73, 110–11, 164
Canterbury Tales, The (Chaucer), 29, 40
Carbury, Sir Felix, 121

192

Carbury, Lady Matilda, 120
Carbury, Roger, 119, 121
'Change Alley, 81, 106
Charles II, king of England, 76
Chaucer, Geoffrey, 14, 29-30, 39, 42, 162, 170; attitude toward medieval church, 32, 34-36, 38, 40-41; toward pilgrims in *Canterbury Tales*, 31-32, 35, 40; toward Lady Prioress, 29-30, 32-36. Works: *Pardoner's Tale*, 100; *Prioresses Tale*, 14, 16-17, 37-38, 41, 43, 132, 162-63; *Shipman's Tale*, 31
Cholmondeley, 143-45
Cibber, Theophilus, *Harlot's Progress, The*, 86
Clarissa (Richardson), 95-97, 166
Codlingsby (Thackeray), 115-16, 168
Cohen, Ezra, 117
Cohen, Jacob, 123
Cohenlupe, Samuel, 120-21
Coleridge, Samuel Taylor, 101, 104, 166; *Rime of the Ancient Mariner, The*, 101
Collected Essays (Orwell), 157-58
Colleoni, 145-46
Commonwealth of Oceana, The (Harrington), 73-74
Congreve, William, *Way of the World, The*, 86
Coningsby (Disraeli), 114, 117
Conscience of the Rich, The (Snow), 154-56, 170
Corridors of Power (Snow), 156-57, 170
Coverley, Sir Roger de, 81
Cowley, Abraham, 70, 164. *See also* Jews, conversion of
Cresson, Warder, 115
Cromwell, Oliver, 14-15, 17, 73-76, 111, 164. *See also* Jews and readmission to England; Jews and the uses of wealth
Crowder, Anne, 143-44, 150
Crusoe, Robinson, 90-92
Cumberland, Richard, *The Jew*, 87, 166

Cunningham, Martin, 133
Curll, Edmund, 88

Dancy, Ronald, 150-52
Daniel Deronda (Eliot), 117-19, 123, 168
Decline and Fall (Waugh), 148
Dedalus, Stephen, 130, 132, 136, 139-41, 153
Dedlock, Lord Leicester and Lady, 113
Defoe, Daniel, 90-91, 95, 99, 111, 165; *Roxana; Or, The Fortunate Mistress*, 91. *See also* Image of the Jew as rogue
DeLevis, Ferdinand, 150-52
Deronda, Daniel, 117-19
Diary of Samuel Pepys, 77-78
Dickens, Charles: dislike of aristocrats, 112-14; and evils of wealth, 15, 104-7, 109-12, 118, 132, 166-67. Works: *Bleak House*, 113-14; *Dombey and Son*, 106-7; *Hard Times*, 107-8, 112; *Little Dorrit*, 109; *Martin Chuzzlewit*, 106; *Old Curiosity Shop*, 105-6; *Oliver Twist*, 15-16, 105-6; *Our Mutual Friend*, 109-10, 113, 167. *See also* Image of the Jew as dandy; Image of the Jew as devil; Image of the Jew as manipuator of wealth and power
Dignam, Paddy, 130, 133
Disraeli, Benjamin, 113; racist comprehensions of, 15, 114, 115, 122, 167-68. Works: *Coningsby*, 114, 117; *Endymion*, 117; *Tancred*, 114-15, 168
Dombey and Son (Dickens), 106-7
Dombey, Paul, Sr., 106-7
Donne, John, 17, 67-68, 164. *See also* Jews, conversion of
Dover Beach (Arnold), 141-42
Dorrit, William, 109
Dryden, John, 17, 85, 165; *Love Triumphant*, 85
Duenna, The (Sheridan), 86
Du Maurier, George: racist comprehensions of (in *Trilby*), 123, 168

Eliot, George, 15, 122, 132, 154; racist comprehensions of, 117, 122–23, 168; *Daniel Deronda*, 117–19, 123, 168
Eliot, Lewis, 153–57
Elizabeth I, queen of England, 43
Emilius, Joseph ("Jew-priest"), 116–17, 167
Endymion (Disraeli), 117
Essay on Man (Pope), 89
Eva, 114–15, 168
Evelyn, John, 76

Fagan, Dr. Augustus, 148
Fagin, 15, 102, 104–7, 109, 111, 122; as paradigm for Dickens's later villains, 15, 104–5, 109. *See also* Image of the Jew as devil; Image of the Jew as manipulator of wealth and power
Ferdinand, Count Fathom (Smollett), 94–95, 166
Filippo Baldinucci on the Privilege of Burial (Browning), 125
Fielding, Henry, 86, 165; *Miss Lucy in Town*, 86
Fisker, Hamilton K., 121
Flanders, Moll, 91
Fledgeby, Fascination, 112–13
Friar, 31–32

Galsworthy, John, 16, 19, 152–53, 169–70; *Loyalties*, 149–53, 169. *See also* Image of the Jew as status-seeker
Getliffe, Francis, 155–56
Getliffe, Katherine (March), 155–57
Gideon, Sampson, 82–83
Gilman, Mr., 151, 156
Goldstein, Emanuel, 159–60, 170
Gosson, Stephen, 47
Gower, John, *Confessio Amantis*, 17
Gradgrind, Louisa, 108
Grandcort, Henleigh, 118
Granville, George, *Jew of Venice, The*, 85
Gratiano, 51, 54–55, 57
Gratz, Rebecca, 97
Great chain of being, 25, 60, 89

Greene, Graham, 16, 19, 142–44, 153. Works: *Brighton Rock*, 16, 142, 146–48; *This Gun for Hire*, 142–46, 148, 153; *Orient Express*, 148. *See also* Image of the Jew as betrayer; Image of the Jew as manipulator of wealth and power

Hale, Fred, 146
Hard Times (Dickens), 107–8, 112
Harleth, Gwendolen, 118
Harlot's Progress, The (Cibber), 86
Harrington, James, *Commonwealth of Oceana, The*, 73
Harthouse, James, 108, 112–13, 167. *See also* Image of the Jew as dandy
Hazlitt, William, 122
Heartbreak House (Shaw), 129
Helena (Waugh), 168
Henry III, king of England, 37
Herbert of Cherbury, Edward, Lord, 66
Herbert, of George, 69. *See also* Jews, conversion of
Hobbes, Thomas, *Leviathan*, 67
Holy-Cross Day (Browning), 125
Hugh of Lincoln legend, 37–39, 132
Humphrey Clinker (Smollett), 94

Image of the Jew: as alien, 15–16, 41, 90, 131–34, 136–40, 152–53, 160–61, 169; as betrayer, 142–47; as dandy, 85–86, 108, 112–13, 116–17, 165, 167; as devil, 14–15, 24–25, 29, 43, 63, 91–93, 97, 105–6, 163–64; as manipulator of wealth and power, 15–16, 45, 47–52, 56–57, 82, 86, 90–96, 99, 102, 104–7, 109–112, 116, 118, 120–22, 128–29, 138–39, 143–44, 147, 155–56, 163–70; as peculiar personality, 79, 84–87, 90, 95, 110–12, 165–66; as rogue, 90, 93–95; as status-seeker, 85–86, 150–51, 156, 165
Irving, Washington, 97
Isaac of York, 97, 99–100
Ivanhoe (Scott), 18, 96–100
Ivanhoe, Wilfred of, 97–99

Index

Jessica, 45, 51, 57-60, 62, 97, 100, 121
Jew, The (Cumberland), 87, 166
Jew, The (Gosson's reference), 47
Jew of Malta. *See* Barabas
Jew of Malta, The (Marlowe), 17, 44-46, 163-64, 170
Jews: as aliens, 14, 24-25, 42, 89, 122, 157-58, 160, 162-63, 165-66, 168-69; attitude of medieval church toward, 13-14, 23-28, 36-41, 162-64; conversion of, 14, 24, 27, 40, 42, 47, 67-70, 100, 164-66; eighteenth-century attitudes toward, 81-87, 90-91, 94, 100, 102, 165; Puritan attitudes toward, 74-76, 78-80, 164; and readmission to England, 17, 75-76; sentimental attitudes toward, 18, 87, 94, 164-65; and the uses of wealth, 25-26, 73-76, 82-84, 91, 162-66; Victorian attitudes toward, 15-16, 104, 109-12, 114-19, 121-23
Jochanan Hakkadosh (Browning), 125
Joyce, James, 16, 19, 129, 131-33, 135-36, 140-42, 149, 170; *Ulysses*, 16, 96, 129-42
Julia, 160
Jupe, Sissy, 108

Kiernan, Barney, 132, 135-36, 139
Klesmer, Herr, 119
"Mr. Know-All" (Maugham), 149

Lammle, Mr. and Mrs. Alfred, 110
Langland, William, *Vision concerning Piers the Plowman, The*, 17
Lawrence, Brother, 124
Lazarus, 170
Lazarus and Undershaft, 128-29
Lewes, George Henry, 118
Levy, Benjamin, 82
Lismahago, Obadiah, 94
Little Dorrit (Dickens), 109
Little Nell, 105
Love à la Mode (Macklin), 86
Love Triumphant (Dryden), 85
Loyalties (Galsworthy), 149-53, 156, 169

Macaulay, Thomas Babington, 122
Macklin, Charles, *Love à la Mode*, 86
Major Barbara (Shaw), 128-29, 143
Man and Superman (Shaw), 128
Manasseh, Joshua, 94-95
March, Charles, 155-56
March, Leonard, 155-56
Marcus, Sir, 142-44, 170
Marlowe, Christopher, 44-45, 82, 163, 170; *Jew of the Malta, The*, 17, 44-46, 163-64, 170
Martin Chuzzlewit (Dickens), 106
Mather, Jimmy, 143, 145
Maugham, W. Somerset, 16, 19, 149, 169; "Mr. Know-All," 149; *Razor's Edge, The*, 149
Medina, Solomon, 82
Melmotte, Augustus, 109, 120-22, 167. *See also* Image of the Jew as manipulator of wealth and power
Melmotte, Marie, 121
Melvil, 95
Men at Arms (Waugh), 149
Mendoza, 128, 153. *See also* Image of the Jew as devil
Mendoza, Isaac, 86
Mendoza, Miriam, 115-16, 168
Mendoza, Rafael, 116
Mercadore, 46
Merceda, Solomon, 95. *See also* Image of the Jew as rogue
Merchant of Venice, The, 14, 16-17, 45-47, 51-52, 63-64, 100, 163-64
Merdle, Mr., 109, 144
"merrie sporte," 47-48, 52, 61. *See also* Image of the Jew as manipulator of wealth and power
Milton, John, 17, 65, 68, 70-74, 78, 84-85, 164. Works: *Of Christian Doctrine*, 71; *Paradise Lost*, 71
Mirah, 119
Monk, 31
Monmouth, Lord, 117
Montague, Paul, 121
Mordecai, 118-19
Moses, 86
My Last Duchess (Browning), 124

Nerissa, 55
1984 (Orwell), 158–61, 170
Notes of a Journey . . . (Thackeray) 115

O'Brien, 159–60
Of Christian Doctrine (Milton), 71
Old Curiosity Shop, The (Dickens), 105–6
Oliver Twist (Dickens), 15, 16, 104–6
O'Molloy, J. J., 137
Orwell, George, 16, 19; attitude toward anti-Semitism, 157–58; attitude toward uses of power, 158–60, 170. Works: *Collected Essays*, 157–58; *1984*, 158–61, 170
Our Mutual Friend (Dickens), 109–10, 113, 167
Orient Express (Greene), 148

Paradise Lost (Milton), 71
Pardoner's Tale, The (Chaucer), 32, 100
Pepys, Samuel, *Diary*, 77–78
Peregrine Pickle (Smollett), 93
Podsnap, Mr. and Mrs. John, 110
Pope, Alexander, 17, 88–89, 165; *Essay on Man*, 89
Portia, 44, 47, 50–51, 53–55, 59–61, 63, 163
Puritanism, 60, 68, 70, 72–74, 78, 90–91, 164–65; and the uses of wealth, 73, 90–91, 164–65
Prioresses Tale, The (Chaucer), 14, 16–17, 37, 41, 43, 132, 162–63; critical evaluations of, 39–40
Purefoy, Mrs. Mina, 130, 136, 140

Quilp, Daniel, 105–6

Rapine, Isaac, 93–94
Raven, James, 143–44, 153
Razor's Edge, The (Maugham), 149
Rebecca, 96–100, 166
Riah, Mr., 111–12
Richard I, king of England, 27, 98–99
Richardson, Samuel, 96, 165, 166. Works: *Sir Charles Grandison*, 95–

97; *Clarissa*, 95–97, 166
Rime of the Ancient Mariner, The (Coleridge), 101
Ring and the Book, The (Browning), 125
Roderick Random (Smollett), 93
Rothschild, Father, S.J., 148–49
Rowena, 99
Roxana; Or, The Fortunate Mistress (Defoe), 90–92
Rubin, David, 156

St. Barbe, 117
Salanio and Salerio, 51–52
Sancho, 85
School for Scandal, The (Sheridan), 88
Scott, Sir Walter, *Ivanhoe*, 18, 96–100, 166
Shakespeare, William, 42, 46–47, 50–52, 63, 132, 163–64; *Merchant of Venice, The*, 14, 16–17, 45–47, 51–52, 63–64, 163–64
Sharp, Rebecca, 117
Shaw, George Bernard, 15–16, 19, 128–29, 143, 152, 169. Works: *Heartbreak House*, 129; *Major Barbara*, 128–29, 143; *Man and Superman*, 128
Shelley, Percy Bysshe, 101
Sheridan, Richard Brinsley: *Duenna, The*, 86; *School for Scandal, The*, 86
Sheva, 87
Shipman's Tale, The (Chaucer), 31
Shylock: as devil, 14, 63; humanization of, 49, 57, 61–62; as moneylender, 47–51; as sober merchant, 56–57, 164; unfitted for Belmont, 57, 59–61; as usurer, 14, 97, 99; as villain, 45, 52, 58–59, 63, 163–64
Sidonia, 114–17, 167. *See also* Image of the Jew as manipulator of wealth and power.
Singleton, Captain, 91
Sir Charles Grandison (Richardson), 95–97
Smith, John, 65–66
Smith, Winston, 159–60

Smollett, Tobias, 87, 92-95, 99, 165-66. Works: *Ferdinand, Count Fathom*, 87, 94-95, 166; *Humphrey Clinker*, 92-94; *Peregrine Pickle*, 93; *Roderick Random*, 93
Snow, Charles P., 19, 153-54, 156-57, 160, 170. Works: *Conscience of the Rich, The*, 154-56, 170; *Corridors of Power*, 156-57, 170. See also Image of the Jew as manipulator of wealth and power
Southey, Robert, 101
Sparsit, Mrs., 108-9
Stanhope, Ethelbert, 116
Stephen-Joyce-Telemachus, 139
Summoner, 32
Swift, Jonathan, 17, 87, 89, 95, 129

Tancred (Disraeli), 114-15, 167
Tancred, Lord Montacute, 113-15, 117
Tanner, Jack, 128, 153
Taylor, Jeremy, 68, 78
Templeton, Elliott, 149
Thackeray, William Makepeace, 15, 116-18, 166-68. Works: *Codlingsby*, 115-16, 168; *Notes of a Journey from Cornhill to Grand Cairo*, 115, 168; *Vanity Fair*, 117-18
This Gun for Hire (Greene), 142-46, 148, 153
Three Ladies of London (Robert Wilson), 46
Trollope, Anthony, 15, 118, 120, 132, 154, 167. Works: *Barchester Towers*, 116, 168; *Eustace Diamonds, The*, 116-17, 168; *Way We Live Now, The*, 109, 119-21, 167
Twisden, Jacob, 152
Twist, Oliver, 105-7

Ulysses, 130-33, 137, 139
Ulysses (Joyce), 16, 129-42
Ulysses-Bloom, 141
Ulysses-Bloom-God, 140
Undershaft, Andrew, 143

Vanity Fair (Thackeray), 117, 167
Vaughan, Henry, 69-70. See also Jews, conversion of
Veneering, Mr. and Mrs. Hamilton, 110
Venice: contrast with Belmont, 57, 59-61, 64

Wandering Jew, legend of, 18, 100-101, 166
Waugh, Evelyn, 19, 169. Works: *Decline and Fall*, 148; *Helena*, 149; *Men at Arms*, 149; *Vile Bodies*, 148
Way of the World, The (Congreve), 86
William IV, king of England, 84
Williams, Roger, *Bloody Tenent of Persecution, The*, 73
Wilson, Robert, *Three Ladies of London*, 46
Winsor, Charles, 151
Winsor, Lady Adela, 151
Wordsworth, William, 166